T0265645

Enchanted Baking

Enchanted Baking

Thibaud Villanova

PHOTOGRAPHY
Nicolas Lobbestaël

STYLING
Mehdiya Kerairia

TRANSLATION
Lisa Molle Troyer

INSIGHT **I** EDITIONS

SAN RAFAEL · LOS ANGELES · LONDON

I'm so delighted to be joining you on another deliciously enchanted journey through the greatest Disney and Pixar films!

Welcome to my latest cookbook. I've devised and written nearly twenty cookbooks since my very first one was published in 2014. My philosophy and work are simple: I design recipes that anyone can follow, inspired by the most popular fictional worlds. My books also channel those worlds with photography and artistic design, inviting you to inhabit your favorite films, TV shows, books, and games. This cookbook was created with the same passion, energy, and love of food I always pour into my books—and you'll know exactly what that means if you've read the others!

Let me reassure those of you with less experience in the kitchen that I design recipes simple enough for you to re-create at home and enjoy the results! That's why this book provides detailed recipe directions, pictures of every recipe, and simple instructions with step-by-step photos for the basic skills you'll need. I fully believe that you will be able to complete every one of the recipes in this book.

Just like *Disney Enchanted Recipes*, which was released in English in 2022, this cookbook takes you on an adventure—this time a quest for honeyed pastries, dreamy cakes, and fruity treats. Revisit your favorite Disney animated films with these enchanted desserts as you create a fantastical spread of sugary delights. These pages contain a chocolate hazelnut cake like the one Geppetto bakes for Cleo; a deliciously enticing version of the spelled apple from Snow White; a sumptuous wedding cake like the one served to Ariel, the little mermaid; a spiced fruit tea straight out of Kumandra; ginger cookies like those Penny eats while waiting for Bernard and Bianca to rescue her; desserts befitting the Beast's dining table; and many other surprises, each more mouthwatering than the last.

So welcome, Disney fans—beginners and experienced bakers alike—to a world of sweet imagination. I hope you enjoy all the subtle references (and find the Easter eggs) I've hidden throughout this book. I hope you have fun cooking for yourself and for your friends and family. And I hope that reading these pages puts a smile on your face!

Enjoy the book!

Thibaud Villanova
Gastronogeek

UTENSILS

Hand mixer

Saucepan

Strainer

Bread knife

Paring knife

Chef's knife

Wooden spoon

Mixing bowl

Cupcake filling tip

Fluted tip

Round tip

Vegetable peeler

Round cookie cutter

Whisk

Waffle maker
(or waffle iron)

Bowl scraper

Wire rack

Ladle

Silicone spatula

Measuring spoons

Blender

Immersion blender

Springform pan

Muffin tin

Ice pop mold

Pie plate

Bundt pan

Steamer basket

Pastry brush

Silicone baking mat

Piping bag

Frying pan

Pie weights

Stand mixer

Rolling pin

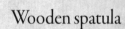

Wooden spatula

Cake writing gel

Cooking thermometer

Liquid measuring cup

Zester

CONTENTS

P RINCESS
FIT FOR A

SNOW WHITE AND
THE SEVEN DWARFS
WISHING APPLE
Candy apple with rosemary
p. 14

STEP BY STEP
Red Caramel
p. 16

CINDERELLA
BREAKFAST TIME PORRIDGE
Rolled oats, lavender honey, pistachios,
and apricot jam
p. 19

BEAUTY AND THE BEAST
BE OUR GUEST PARIS-BREST
Choux pastry with praline crème mousseline
p. 20

BEASTLY CRÊPES SUZETTE
Crêpes Suzette with flambéed orange supremes
p. 24

TANGLED
TOWER COOKIES
Gooey chocolate chip cookies
with macadamia nuts
p. 26

BRAVE
TRANSFORMATION SPELL CAKE
Blueberry pie with almond cream and
thistle honey
p. 28

THE PRINCESS AND
THE FROG
BANANAS FOSTER FOR LOUIS
Flambéed bananas with pecans, rum,
and vanilla ice cream
p. 30

THE LITTLE MERMAID
ROYAL WEDDING CAKE
Rose cake with vanilla whipped cream
p. 32

GLOBAL CUISINE

PINOCCHIO
A CAKE FOR CLEO
Orange cake with
chocolate hazelnut icing
p. 38

STEP BY STEP
Cutting a Cake into Layers
p. 42

STEP BY STEP
Chocolate Ganache
p. 44

STEP BY STEP
Chocolate Hazelnut Icing
p. 46

LADY AND THE TRAMP
DOUGHNUTS FOR LADY
Strawberry jelly doughnuts
p. 48

THE JUNGLE BOOK
BARE NECESSITIES LASSI
Spiced mango yogurt drink
p. 52

THE ARISTOCATS
ROQUEFORT'S DELIGHT
Vanilla cream and cookies
p. 54

BIG HERO 6
LUCKY CAT CAFÉ
NEKO MUFFINS
Blackberry matcha muffins
p. 58

COCO
MARIGOLD BRIDGE PAN
DE MUERTO
Sweet buns with
orange blossom water
p. 60

THE RESCUERS
PENNY'S COOKIES
Ginger cookies
p. 62

CHIP 'N' DALE
ANIMATED SHORTS
PANCAKE BREAKFAST
Homemade vanilla pancakes
p. 64

UP
ADVENTURE IS OUT
THERE ICE CREAM
Vanilla almond and chocolate
hazelnut nice cream
p. 67

LUCA
PORTOROSSO CANNOLI
Ricotta and pistachio cannoli
p. 68

ENCANTO
MAMA MADRIGAL'S
BUÑUELOS
Sweet cheese fritters
p. 71

BAO
SWEET BAO
Dumplings with red bean paste
p. 72

STEP BY STEP
Folding Bao
p. 74

LILO & STITCH
ONE EXTRATERRESTRIAL
BITE CAKE
Black forest cake
p. 76

MEET THE ROBINSONS
IT'S JAMMED!
EXPLOSIVE PB&J
Buttered honeyed peanut butter
and jelly sandwich
p. 78

SOUL
REGULAR OLE LIVING
PECAN PIE
Diner-style pecan pie
p. 80

STEP BY STEP
Blind Baking a Crust
p. 82

CONTENTS

F ANTASY
WORLDS

ZOOTOPIA
PAWPSICLES
Strawberry verbena ice pops
p. 86

CARROT POPS
Candied carrot lollipops
p. 88

MONSTERS UNIVERSITY
RANDALL'S BE MY PAL CUPCAKES
Chocolate cupcakes with vanilla frosting
p. 91

STEP BY STEP
Piping frosting
p. 92

INCREDIBLES 2
MOUSSE FOR JACK-JACK
Blackberry lavender mousse
p. 95

INCREDIBLES 2
EVERYDAY WAFFLES FOR
NOT-SO-EVERYDAY KIDS
Waffles with salted butter and maple syrup
p. 96

HERCULES
HERCULES FAN COLA
Homemade cola with Greek citrus
p. 98

RAYA AND
THE LAST DRAGON
KUMANDRA ICED TEA
Iced tea with jasmine, chile peppers,
lemongrass, and palm sugar
p. 100

LEGENDARY STICKY RICE
Coconut sticky rice with mango
p. 103

SOUL
PIZZA FROM THE GREAT BEYOND
Dessert pizza with fruit, white chocolate,
and almond butter
p. 105

FROZEN
ICED ROYAL CROWN CAKE
Fluffy bundt cake with Seville orange,
orange glaze, and candied ginger
p. 106

T IPS

DOUGHS AND CRUSTS
Pie crust
Shortbread crust
p. 110
Puff pastry
p. 111
Choux pastry
Sweet almond dough
p. 112
Pizza dough
p. 113

CREAMS
Pastry cream
p. 114
Custard
French buttercream
p. 115
Almond cream
Whipped cream
p. 116
Commonly used piping tips
p. 117

ICINGS AND FROSTINGS
Chocolate icing
p. 118
Royal icing
Lemon glaze
Cream cheese frosting
p. 119
Mirror glaze
p. 120

SPONGE CAKES
Joconde sponge cake
Genoise sponge cake
p. 121

CHOCOLATE
Chocolate sauce
Types of chocolate
p. 122
Tempering chocolate
p. 123

SYRUPS AND DESSERT SAUCES
Basic syrup
Light syrup
p. 124
Liquid caramel
Salted butter caramel sauce
p. 125

SPREADS AND BUTTERS
Chocolate hazelnut spread
p. 126
Speculoos cookie butter
Anko paste
p. 127
Pistachio butter
p. 128

MERINGUES
Italian meringue
French meringue
p. 129

ICE CREAMS
Vanilla ice cream
p. 130
Chocolate ice cream
p. 131

SEASONAL FRUITS AND NUTS
p. 132

CONVERSIONS
p. 133

GLOSSARY
p. 134

INDEX
p. 138

FIT FOR A
PRINCESS

WISHING APPLE

CANDY APPLE WITH ROSEMARY

DIFFICULTY: 🍎🍎
PREP TIME: 5 minutes
RESTING TIME: 5 minutes
COOK TIME: 10 minutes

INGREDIENTS

YIELD: 6 SERVINGS

ROSEMARY CARAMEL
½ cup water
1¼ cups granulated sugar
2½ tablespoons light corn syrup
1½ tablespoons butter
1½ tablespoons rosemary syrup
5 drops red food coloring

6 Pink Lady apples

EQUIPMENT

6 wooden skewers
Cooking thermometer (optional)

Snow White wished upon a magic apple, and the Queen's evil plan took hold. Don't worry: This recipe makes an enticing candy apple that is safe to eat—and safe to wish upon!

1. Make the rosemary caramel: Pour the water into a medium saucepan. Add the sugar and corn syrup. Heat the mixture over medium heat to a temperature of 300°F. If you don't have a cooking thermometer, bring the mixture to a boil; then continue cooking it for 10 minutes, keeping a close eye on the saucepan to make sure the mixture doesn't burn.

2. While the caramel is cooking, get ready for the dipping: Wash and dry the apples. Push a wooden skewer into each apple, at least halfway into the fruit. Set a piece of parchment paper (or a greased smooth plate) nearby.

3. Remove the saucepan from heat, and add the butter and rosemary syrup. Stir in the red food coloring. Feel free to add more if you don't think your caramel is a bright enough red. Stir vigorously with a spatula.

4. Immediately dip the apples into the caramel, one by one, to fully coat.

5. Set the apples on the sheet of parchment paper (or the plate), skewer-side up, and let the caramel harden into a tantalizing—even irresistible!—confection.

STEP BY STEP
RED CARAMEL

INGREDIENTS

½ cup water

1¼ cups granulated sugar

2½ tablespoons light corn syrup

1½ tablespoons butter

5 drops red food coloring

1. Pour the water into a medium saucepan. Add the sugar.

2. Add the corn syrup.

3. Heat the mixture to a temperature of 300°F. If you don't have a cooking thermometer, bring the mixture to a boil; then continue cooking it for 10 minutes, keeping a close eye on the saucepan to make sure the mixture doesn't burn.

4. Remove from heat. Add the butter, and stir well.

5. Add the red food coloring.

6. Stir with a wooden spoon or a spatula until the mixture becomes a bright red caramel that is ready to use for coating the apples.

Note:
You can flavor the caramel by adding syrup (about 1½ tablespoons). You can also make caramel of any color by using other food colorings or combining several of them. Feel free to add more than 5 drops if you want a brighter color.

BREAKFAST TIME PORRIDGE

ROLLED OATS, LAVENDER HONEY, PISTACHIOS, AND APRICOT JAM

DIFFICULTY:
PREP TIME: 15 minutes
COOK TIME: 10 minutes
RESTING TIME: 15 minutes

INGREDIENTS

YIELD: 4 SERVINGS

2 cups almond milk

3⅓ cups rolled oats

2 teaspoons lavender honey, divided, plus more as desired

2 tablespoons pistachio butter

4 teaspoons apricot jam

5 tablespoons shelled pistachios

Cinderella greeted each morning with an apron full of seeds for the birds and mice. Start your day with this hearty porridge of oats, nuts, and jam, and you, too, will be singing while you do your chores.

1. Pour the almond milk into a large saucepan, and bring to a boil.

2. Turn down the heat to very low, and add the oats and 1 teaspoon honey. Cook the oats for 10 minutes, stirring continuously.

3. Remove the saucepan from heat, and mix in the pistachio butter. Cover, and let rest for 15 minutes before plating.

To plate:
Divide the porridge among 4 bowls. To each bowl, add 1 teaspoon apricot jam, a few pistachios, and, if desired, an additional drizzle of honey to sweeten. Serve with a hot cup of black tea.

Note:
You can make this recipe vegan by using maple or agave syrup instead of honey. Also try experimenting with different combinations of nuts and jam.

BE OUR GUEST PARIS-BREST

CHOUX PASTRY WITH PRALINE CRÈME MOUSSELINE

DIFFICULTY: 🕯️🕯️🕯️

PREP TIME: 30 minutes

COOK TIME: 1 hour

RESTING TIME: 30 minutes

INGREDIENTS

YIELD: 4 SERVINGS

CHOUX PASTRY

1 cup plus 2 tablespoons water, divided

7 tablespoons butter

1 teaspoon salt

1⅔ cups flour

4 eggs plus 1 egg yolk, divided

1 cup sliced almonds

PRALINE CRÈME MOUSSELINE

1 cup whole milk

3 egg yolks

2 tablespoons sugar

3¼ tablespoons cornstarch

5 tablespoons butter

½ cup praline paste (or almond paste), divided

Powdered sugar, for dusting

With pride, pleasure, and an abundance of charm, Lumière, Cogsworth, and all the dishes welcome Belle to the castle table. Invite your friends to be your guest when you dish out this classic French pastry.

1. Preheat the oven to 350°F.

2. Make the choux pastry: Pour 1 cup water into a medium saucepan, and add the butter. Set the saucepan over medium heat, stir as the butter melts, and bring the mixture to a gentle boil. Remove from heat, and add the salt and the flour all at once. Stir with a spatula until you have a thick, smooth paste with no lumps. This paste is called the panade. Return the saucepan to the stove, and set the panade over medium heat. Continue to stir until it dries out and becomes a dough that pulls away from the sides of the saucepan.

3. Let the dough cool to room temperature, and then transfer to a large mixing bowl. Beat in the 4 eggs one at a time, making sure each is fully incorporated before adding the next—this is critical for a good pastry dough. Continue to mix until the batter is smooth and even and flows in thick ribbons.

4. Set out a silicone baking mat with measurements, or trace an 8-inch circle on a sheet of parchment paper. Place the mat or paper on a baking sheet.

5. Transfer the choux pastry to a piping bag fitted with a large round tip. Pipe a ring of batter along the marked circle. Pipe a second ring just inside and touching the first ring so that the two stick together. Finally, pipe a third ring on top of the first two, nestled into the groove between the two rings.

6. In a small bowl, mix the egg yolk with 2 tablespoons water. Using a pastry brush, delicately brush a little of the egg wash over the surface of the dough, to help it brown in the oven. Take care to not let the egg wash run. Sprinkle sliced almonds over top.

7. Bake for 12 minutes. Then turn off the oven, use a wooden spoon to crack open the oven door slightly, and let the pastry wreath continue to bake for another 35 minutes.

8. Remove the pastry from the oven, and set it on a wire rack until you are ready to assemble the dessert.

EQUIPMENT

3 piping bags with
1 large round tip and 1 fluted tip

Pastry brush

Silicone baking mat
with measurements
(or parchment paper)

9. Make the Praline Crème Mousseline: Pour the milk into a medium sauce-pan, and bring to a simmer. Add the egg yolks, sugar, and cornstarch to a large mixing bowl. Whisk vigorously until the mixture is frothy and lighter in color. Pour one third of the simmering milk into the mixing bowl, and whisk vigorously to combine without cooking the eggs. Pour the entire contents of the mixing bowl back into the saucepan with the remaining milk, and whisk to thoroughly combine all the ingredients. Continue whisking until the mixture thickens. Turn off the heat once the milk begins to simmer.

10. Cut the butter into pieces, and add it to the saucepan, whisking continuously. Whisk in ¼ cup praline (or almond) paste. Transfer the resulting crème mousseline into a piping bag fitted with a fluted tip. Refrigerate for 30 minutes before assembling the pastry.

11. Meanwhile, transfer the remaining ¼ cup praline (or almond) paste into a separate piping bag. Set aside.

To assemble:
Slice the pastry wreath horizontally into 2 equal parts. Generously pipe your crème mousseline over the bottom layer using the first piping bag. At regular intervals, poke the tip of the second piping bag into the crème mousseline, and inject small quantities of praline paste into the mousseline. Cover the filling with the top layer of pastry, dust with powdered sugar, and enjoy!

BEASTLY CRÊPES SUZETTE

CRÊPES SUZETTE WITH FLAMBÉED ORANGE SUPREMES

Here's a recipe for a classic sweet crêpe topped with a fired-up flambéed sauce—a pairing inspired by sweet Belle and the fiery Beast.

DIFFICULTY:
PREP TIME: 30 minutes
RESTING TIME: 1 hour
COOK TIME: 10 minutes,
plus 1½ minutes per crêpe

INGREDIENTS

YIELD: 4 SERVINGS

CRÊPES

½ cup sugar

6 eggs

1 teaspoon vanilla extract

4 cups flour, divided

2¼ cups whole milk, divided

2 cups water

1½ tablespoons salted butter,
melted and cooled

Salt

Sunflower oil, for cooking

SUZETTE SAUCE

½ cup sugar

6 Valencia oranges

3½ tablespoons butter

1 teaspoon orange liqueur

1 teaspoon lemon juice

½ cup sliced almonds (optional),
for serving

⅔ cup Grand Marnier,
for serving

1. Make the crêpe batter: Always add the ingredients in this order, and you'll never have lumpy batter: Add the sugar, eggs, and vanilla extract to a large mixing bowl. Whisk vigorously for 1½ to 2 minutes. Whisk in 2 cups of the flour and then the remaining 2 cups, to form a fairly dry mixture. Pour in the milk one third at a time, whisking to incorporate each new addition, until the batter is smooth and creamy. Do the same with the water. Finally, stir in the butter and a pinch of salt. Cover the surface with plastic wrap, and refrigerate for at least 1 hour.

2. Meanwhile, make the Suzette sauce: Add the sugar to a medium mixing bowl. Zest the oranges into the bowl of sugar. Stir well, to help the sugar absorb the flavor of the orange zest. Use a paring knife to cut 2 of the oranges into supremes (segments without peel and pith), and set aside. Squeeze the juice from the remaining 4 oranges into a medium saucepan, and add the zest-infused sugar. Bring to a simmer over medium heat, and cook until the sugar has dissolved and the contents have reduced by half, about 10 minutes.

3. Cube the butter, and add it into the orange juice reduction. Stirring continuously, cook over medium heat for another 5 minutes to reduce. Stir in the orange liqueur and lemon juice. Pour the mixture through a strainer into a bowl, and set aside the liquid until you are ready to plate.

4. Warm a crêpe pan over medium heat, and coat it with a drizzle of sunflower oil. When the pan is hot, pour in a small ladleful of batter. Tilt the pan to coat the entire cooking surface with batter, and then return it to heat. As soon as the edges of the crêpe release from the pan, flip it and cook the other side for 20 seconds. Transfer your first crêpe to a plate, and cover. Repeat until you have used all the batter.

To plate:
For each guest, fold 3 crêpes into triangles, and arrange them in the center of a plate. Pour a little Suzette sauce over the top, garnish with a few orange supremes, and sprinkle with sliced almonds. Pour the Grand Marnier into a small saucepan, and warm it over high heat. Use a long match to ignite the liquor, and then pour the flaming liquid over the crêpes. Enjoy!

TOWER COOKIES

GOOEY CHOCOLATE CHIP COOKIES WITH MACADAMIA NUTS

DIFFICULTY: ☀
PREP TIME: 10 minutes
RESTING TIME: 1 hour
COOK TIME: 10 minutes

INGREDIENTS

YIELD: 4 SERVINGS

⅔ cup whole macadamia nuts
1¼ cups flour
1 teaspoon baking powder
½ teaspoon baking soda
Salt
5 tablespoons salted butter
½ cup brown sugar
1 egg
½ cup milk chocolate chip

Every morning at 7 a.m., Rapunzel starts her day. She practices sketching, pottery, dancing, reading, chess, and baking, all while daydreaming of the world outside her tower. Mix up a batch of these delicious cookies, and the aroma of their baking might just send your mind wondering about an adventure of a lifetime, too.

1. Roughly chop the macadamia nuts.

2. Make the cookie dough: In a medium mixing bowl, combine the flour, baking powder, baking soda, and a pinch of salt.

3. In a large mixing bowl, use a silicone spatula to cream together the butter and brown sugar. Stir the egg into the brown sugar mixture, and then add the dry ingredients from the first bowl.

4. Mix for 1 minute; then fold in half the chocolate chips and macadamia nuts. Your cookie dough is ready! Cover the bowl with plastic wrap, and refrigerate for 1 hour.

5. Preheat the oven to 350°F. Line a baking sheet with parchment paper. Remove the cookie dough from the refrigerator. Use your hands to form balls of dough the size of a table tennis ball. Arrange the dough balls on the baking sheet, leaving 2 inches between them. Press the remaining chocolate chips and macadamia nuts into the surface of the dough, and then bake for 10 minutes.

6. Remove the cookies from the oven: They should be gooey in the center and golden brown around the edges. Let cool slightly on the baking sheet before serving.

TRANSFORMATION SPELL CAKE

BLUEBERRY PIE WITH ALMOND CREAM AND THISTLE HONEY

DIFFICULTY:
PREP TIME: 20 minutes
COOK TIME: 50 minutes

INGREDIENTS

YIELD: 6 SERVINGS

11 ounces shortbread crust
(see Tip on page 110)

VANILLA ALMOND CREAM

½ cup plus 1 tablespoon butter,
at room temperature

½ cup sugar

2 teaspoons vanilla extract

3 eggs

1 cup almond flour

BLUEBERRY THISTLE JAM

1 cup fresh blueberries

⅓ cup sugar

2 tablespoons thistle honey

1 tablespoon lemon juice

Powdered sugar, for dusting

EQUIPMENT

Piping bag
Pie weights (or dry beans)

Merida's sneaky little brothers have a reputation for indulging in sweet baked goods. It's no surprise the boys were tempted by the spelled cake, so Merida, naturally, recognized them right away when they revealed themselves as newly formed bear cubs. With this recipe, tastes of the forest are transformed into a sweet delight: a blueberry pie with an Irish countryside shortbread crust.

1. Preheat the oven to 350°F. Pinch off and set aside about a quarter of the shortbread crust (3 ounces). Roll out the rest of the shortbread crust (8 ounces), and press it into a small pie dish. Prick the dough with a fork, and lay a piece of parchment paper over it. Weight down the crust with pie weights (or dry beans), to prevent it from puffing up (*see Step by Step on page 82*). Blind bake the crust for 15 minutes, and then let cool slightly.

2. Make the vanilla almond cream: In a large bowl, beat the butter with a silicone spatula until creamy; then add the sugar and vanilla extract. Add the eggs, one at a time. Whisk to form a smooth cream, and then stir in the almond flour. Transfer the almond cream to a piping bag. Generously fill the pie crust with the contents of the piping bag.

3. Make the blueberry thistle jam: Add the blueberries, sugar, honey, and lemon juice to a medium saucepan. Set the saucepan over medium heat, and cook for 20 minutes to soften the fruit. Spoon a nice, thick scoop of jam into the center of the almond cream filling.

4. Roll out the reserved 3 ounces of pie crust into a disc. Cut a hole in the center, to let the jam show through. Add the top crust to the pie, crimp the outer edge to seal, and bake for 15 minutes.

To plate:
Dust the pie with powdered sugar, and serve generous slices with a hot cup of tea!

BANANAS FOSTER FOR LOUIS

FLAMBÉED BANANAS WITH PECANS, RUM, AND VANILLA ICE CREAM

DIFFICULTY: ❦
PREP TIME: 10 minutes
COOK TIME: 10 minutes

INGREDIENTS

YIELD: 4 SERVINGS

½ cup salted butter

4 very ripe bananas

½ cup brown sugar

2 teaspoons ground cinnamon

20 whole pecans

⅔ cup dark rum

4 speculoos cookies, crushed

4 scoops vanilla ice cream, homemade (see Tip on page 130) or storebought

Louis the alligator yearns for the opportunity to play music with the amazing human musicians of New Orleans. He craves the New Orleans cuisine, too—like crawfish smothered in rémoulade sauce and Bananas Foster sprinkled with pralines.

1. Cut the butter into pieces, and add it to a large frying pan or sauté pan. Melt the butter over medium heat. While the butter is melting, peel the bananas and slice them in half lengthwise. When the butter is melted and hot, add the bananas to the pan, and sprinkle the brown sugar and cinnamon over them. Sauté the bananas for 8 minutes, turning often. Monitor the heat in the pan to make sure the sugar and cooking juices do not burn.

2. Add the pecans. Cook for another 2 minutes, until the bananas are very soft and nicely caramelized.

3. Pour the rum over the bananas and sauce; then use a match to carefully ignite the rum and flambé the alcohol. The bananas will be set ablaze, the alcohol will evaporate, and the bananas and caramel will be infused with the flavors of the rum.

To plate:
Serve 1 banana per person. Spoon caramel from the pan over top, and add 5 pecans. Sprinkle with the crushed speculoos cookies, and add a big scoop of vanilla ice cream. Serve right away.

ROYAL WEDDING CAKE

ROSE CAKE WITH VANILLA WHIPPED CREAM

DIFFICULTY: 🦀🦀🦀

PREP TIME: 1 hour

COOK TIME: 30 minutes

INGREDIENTS

YIELD: 20 SERVINGS

CAKE LAYERS

3½ tablespoons butter,
plus more for greasing

7 eggs

Salt

1 cup sugar

1 teaspoon vanilla extract

1½ cups plus 2 teaspoons flour

ROSE SYRUP

1 cup sugar

2 cups plus 2 tablespoons water

4 teaspoons rose water

WHIPPED CREAM

10½ cups heavy whipping cream,
very cold

18 ounces mascarpone, very cold

1¾ cups powdered sugar

2 teaspoons vanilla extract

4 drops green food coloring

Sebastian enjoys a quiet moment of reflection while observing Ariel and Eric's wedding—from the top of their wedding cake. Then Chef Louis spots him and chops the cake in half! This tall, sweet cake hints of royalty with its rose-infused syrup, and the cake's height will remind you of Ariel's iconic rise from the sea as she dreams of becoming part of your world.

1. Preheat the oven to 350°F. Set a large mixing bowl in the refrigerator. Grease the 3 springform pans.

2. Make the cake batter: In a small saucepan, melt the butter over low heat, and set aside. Separate the egg yolks from the whites into 2 large mixing bowls. Sprinkle the whites with a pinch of salt, and beat until they form stiff peaks; set aside.

3. Pour the sugar into the bowl with the egg yolks, and whisk until the mixture is thick and lighter in color. Stir in the vanilla extract, and set aside.

4. Sift the flour, and add it gradually to the egg yolk mixture. Fold in the stiff egg whites little by little, to obtain a smooth, creamy texture. Finally, stir in the melted butter. Pour the batter into the cake pans, filling to a matching depth in all pans, and bake for 30 minutes. Remove the cake tiers from the pans, to cool.

5. Make the rose syrup: Add the sugar, water, and rose water to a medium saucepan. Heat until the sugar is melted and the water just starts to boil. Set aside.

6. Make the whipped cream: Take the mixing bowl out of the refrigerator, and pour in the whipping cream and mascarpone. Stir in the powdered sugar and vanilla extract. Using a hand mixer, beat the mixture into a firm whipped cream. Add the 4 drops of green food coloring, and stir in gently with a silicone spatula. Transfer the whipped cream to piping bags.

CAKE DECORATIONS

9 ounces strawberries

3½ ounces raspberries

3½ ounces blueberries

Sugar flowers

EQUIPMENT

3 springform pans: 4-inch,
6-inch, and 8-inch diameter

Hand mixer

Piping bags with plain
and patterned tips

Pastry brush

7. Cut each cake tier into 2 layers (*see Step by Step on page 42*). Use a pastry brush to moisten both halves with the rose syrup. Spread a thick layer of whipped cream over the bottom layer of each tier, and then set the top layer over it.

8. Carefully stack the 3 tiers, from the largest on the bottom to the smallest on the top. Spread the remaining whipped cream over the cake. Use an angled spatula to smooth the cream over the entire surface and sides.

9. Add the finishing touches: Arrange the fresh fruit and sugar flowers to decorate the cake. Your wedding cake is ready!

GLOBAL
CUISINE

A CAKE FOR CLEO

ORANGE CAKE WITH CHOCOLATE HAZELNUT ICING

DIFFICULTY: 🍎🍎
PREP TIME: 20 minutes
COOK TIME: 40 minutes
RESTING TIME: 45 minutes

INGREDIENTS

YIELD: 6 SERVINGS

ORANGE CAKE

¾ cup butter, plus more
for greasing

4 eggs

Salt

¾ cup sugar

1⅔ cups flour

4 teaspoons baking powder

Zest of 1 organic orange

4 teaspoons Cointreau

CHOCOLATE GANACHE

5½ ounces dark
baking chocolate

⅔ cup heavy whipping cream

1 tablespoon powdered sugar

Here's a traditional Italian recipe for orange cake with chocolate hazelnut icing. Inspired by Geppetto's love for his sweet little orange goldfish, this dessert is brimming with love and happiness!

1. Make the cake: Preheat the oven to 350°F. In a medium saucepan, melt the butter over medium heat; then remove from heat and set aside.

2. In 2 large mixing bowls, separate the egg yolks from the egg whites. Add 2 pinches of salt to the egg whites, and use a whisk or a hand mixer to beat until they form stiff peaks. Set aside. Add the sugar to the mixing bowl with the egg yolks, and whisk vigorously until the yolks are thick, frothy, and almost white in color. While stirring, add the following ingredients in this order: flour, baking powder, melted butter, orange zest, and Cointreau. Finally, use a silicone spatula to carefully fold in the egg whites, taking care not to deflate them. The batter should be frothy and airy.

3. Grease the cake pan, and pour in the batter. Bake for 35 to 40 minutes. Take the cake out of the oven, and let it cool before removing it from the pan. Set aside the cake on a wire rack at room temperature while you make the chocolate ganache and the chocolate hazelnut icing.

4. Make the ganache: Crush the chocolate in a medium heatproof mixing bowl. Pour the whipping cream into a small saucepan, and bring to a boil. Pour the hot cream over the chocolate, and stir with a silicone spatula until the mixture is rich and creamy. Stir in the powdered sugar; set aside.

CHOCOLATE HAZELNUT ICING

¾ cup whole blanched hazelnuts

7 ounces dark baking chocolate

2 tablespoons neutral vegetable oil

EQUIPMENT

Hand mixer or whisk

7-inch round springform pan

5. Make the chocolate hazelnut icing: Add the hazelnuts to a medium frying pan, and dry roast them for 1½ minutes; then transfer them to your work surface, and roughly chop them. Crush the chocolate in a medium heat-proof mixing bowl, and set it over a double boiler for 5 minutes until the chocolate has melted. Stir in the vegetable oil and hazelnuts.

6. To assemble the cake: Cut the cake into 2 layers. Spread the ganache over the bottom layer (you can use a piping bag, if you prefer), and then put the top half back on. Set the cake on a rack above a small tray. Evenly pour the chocolate hazelnut icing over the cake so that it fully covers the entire surface. Refrigerate the cake for at least 45 minutes.

To plate:
Take the cake out of the refrigerator 15 to 20 minutes before serving. Cut into generous slices, and enjoy!

Good to know:
You can find step-by-step instructions for making ganache and for icing and cutting a cake into layers on pages 42, 44, and 46.

STEP BY STEP
CUTTING A CAKE
INTO LAYERS

INGREDIENTS
1 round cake (see recipe on page 38)

1. Let the cake cool completely, and set it on a rack in front of you. Use a large serrated knife to slice into the side of the cake.

2. Cut slowly through the cake, keeping the cut completely level so that both halves are the same thickness.

3. Use the knife to lift the top layer, to keep it from breaking.

4. Flip over the top layer onto a dish or plate. Your cake is ready to be filled with ▶ ganache or cream (*see page 44*).

STEP BY STEP
CHOCOLATE GANACHE

INGREDIENTS

5½ ounces chocolate

⅔ cup heavy whipping cream

1 tablespoon powdered sugar

1. Crush the chocolate in a medium heat-proof mixing bowl. Pour the whipping cream into a medium saucepan, and bring to a boil. Pour it immediately over the chocolate.

2. Stir the mixture with a silicone spatula until it's rich and creamy.

3. Mix in the powdered sugar.

4. Stir again until you have a smooth ganache.

Notes:

Ganache is versatile. You can use it between the layers of a cake, frost cookies with it, or coat a cake with it instead of using icing. You can also pipe it over cupcakes; to use it that way, let it cool completely to room temperature before transferring it to a piping bag (*see page 92*). Here, we show you how to use the ganache to fill a cake—a very simple path to a rich dessert!

5. Cut your cake into layers following the instructions on page 42. Set the bottom half of your cake on a rack or dish in front of you. Scoop a generous spoonful of ganache into the center.

6. Use the back of the spoon to spread the ganache evenly over the entire surface. Add more ganache, as needed.

7. The entire surface of the cake should now be covered with a thick layer of ganache.

8. Place the top of the cake over the ganache.

9. Let the ganache rest at room temperature before serving. For an even more decadent cake, you can coat the outside with icing (*see page 46*).

STEP BY STEP

CHOCOLATE HAZELNUT ICING

INGREDIENTS

¾ cup whole blanched hazelnuts
7 ounces dark baking chocolate
2 tablespoons neutral vegetable oil

1. Add the hazelnuts to a frying pan, and dry roast them for 1½ minutes; then transfer them to your work surface, and roughly chop them. Set aside in a small bowl.

2. Crush the chocolate in a mixing bowl, and set it over a double boiler.

3. Let the chocolate melt, stirring continuously so that it melts evenly. You should have a bowl of perfectly smooth melted chocolate.

4. Stir the vegetable oil and hazelnuts into the melted chocolate.

5. Set the cake you are icing on a wire rack above a small tray. Evenly pour the icing over the cake so that it fully covers the entire surface. Refrigerate the cake for at least 45 minutes, to allow the icing to set.

Notes:
You can make pure chocolate icing—just skip the hazelnuts. You can also replace the hazelnuts with pecans, walnuts, or almonds.

The same technique can be used to make a white chocolate or milk chocolate icing.

DOUGHNUTS FOR LADY

STRAWBERRY JELLY DOUGHNUTS

Lady is such a civilized dog: She enjoys a fresh doughnut dipped in coffee in the mornings. Our doughnut has a sweet surprise strawberry filling. Dip the doughnut in hot chocolate, coffee, or tea—or enjoy it just on its own.

DIFFICULTY:

PREP TIME: 15 minutes

RESTING TIME: 1 hour

COOK TIME: 10 minutes

INGREDIENTS

YIELD: 4 DOUGHNUTS

2½ teaspoons active dry yeast

1½ cups plus 1 tablespoon flour, plus more for dusting

1½ tablespoons sugar

Salt

1 egg

⅓ cup milk, at room temperature

3 tablespoons cold butter, chopped

2 cups oil, for frying

4 tablespoons strawberry jam (or your favorite flavor)

Powdered sugar, for dusting

1. Activate the yeast: Pour the yeast into a small cup or glass. Fill the packet with warm water, and pour it over the yeast. Stir, and let rest for 5 minutes.

2. Attach a dough hook to your stand mixer, and use it to combine the flour, sugar, and pinch of salt. Form a well in the dry ingredients.

3. In a separate bowl, beat the egg until frothy. Pour the beaten egg into the well, along with the activated yeast and the milk. Knead the dough for 5 minutes on medium speed until the dough begins to detach from the sides of the bowl. Add the butter, and knead for another 5 minutes.

4. Use a bowl scraper to scoop out the dough and form it into a ball. Set aside for 1 hour in a medium bowl covered with plastic wrap. During this hour of resting time, the active yeast will cause the dough to rise.

5. After the dough has rested, turn it out onto a floured work surface. Press down the dough with your fist to deflate it slightly. Next, form the dough into a thick log, and cut it into 4 equal pieces. Roll each piece between your hands to form a little ball. Use a rolling pin to flatten each dough ball into a circle approximately 1 inch thick. Use the cookie cutter to cut a doughnut hole in the center of each circle.

EQUIPMENT

Stand mixer with dough hook

Round cookie cutter,
1¼-inch diameter

Cooking thermometer

Piping bag with
a cupcake filling tip

6. Set a plate covered with paper towels nearby, with a few more paper towels beside it. In a large high-sided pot or deep fryer, heat the frying oil to 340°F (use a cooking thermometer to check the temperature). Drop the doughnuts into the hot oil, and fry for 4 minutes on each side. When the doughnuts are golden brown, scoop them out of the oil and immediately set them on paper towels, to drain. Pat the surface with more paper towels, to absorb as much of the remaining frying oil as possible.

7. Fill the doughnuts: Transfer the jam to a piping bag fitted with a cupcake filling tip. Poke each doughnut in several places, and inject a little jam. Be careful—if you press too hard, your doughnuts may burst!

To plate:
Dust your doughnuts with powdered sugar, and serve warm.

The Morning Post

THE WEATHER

STROPHE SEE
ISA ROOMS!!

Commission
'oom' Report

xt of MARTI
Report PR
OVER

BARE NECESSITIES LASSI

SPICED MANGO YOGURT DRINK

DIFFICULTY: 🌿

PREP TIME: 5 minutes
RESTING TIME: 30 minutes
COOK TIME: 10 minutes

INGREDIENTS

YIELD: 4 SERVINGS

1⅔ cups milk or almond milk

1 small stick cinnamon

1 star anise

4 cardamom pods

2 very ripe mangoes

2½ cups plain yogurt

1 tablespoon honey

Ice cubes, for serving

Mint leaves, for serving (optional)

EQUIPMENT

Blender

Baloo takes Mowgli on a song-filled tour of the abundant treats of the jungle, pointing out all the juicy, delicious tropical fruits. Here's a way to use one of those fruits for an energizing drink that will make you want to get up and dance.

1. Pour the milk into a medium saucepan. Add the cinnamon stick, star anise, and cardamom pods, and bring to a boil. Remove the saucepan from heat, letting the contents cool to room temperature; steep for 30 minutes.

2. When the spiced milk has cooled and steeped, strain out the spices and set the liquid aside.

3. Peel and pit the mangoes. Add the fruit to a blender, along with the yogurt, spice-infused milk, and honey. Blend on high for 1½ minutes, to get a smooth consistency. Your spiced mango lassi is ready!

To serve:
Add ice cubes and mint leaves for an even more refreshing drink. Enjoy right away.

ROQUEFORT'S DELIGHT

VANILLA CREAM AND COOKIES

DIFFICULTY:

PREP TIME: 20 minutes
RESTING TIME: 45 minutes
COOK TIME: 20 minutes

INGREDIENTS

YIELD: 4 SERVINGS

VANILLA COOKIES

5 tablespoons salted butter,
at room temperature
¼ cup plus 2 tablespoons sugar
2 teaspoons vanilla extract
1 egg
1 cup flour

"Double delicious!" exclaims the friendly mouse Roquefort after dipping his cookie in the sweet, warm milk Edgar prepares for the cats. Delight your friends with the double deliciousness of these homemade cookies and cream.

1. Make the vanilla cookies: In a large mixing bowl, use a silicone spatula to soften the butter; then mix in the sugar and vanilla extract. When the butter and sugar are thoroughly combined, whisk in the egg. Finally, add the flour, and knead to form a ball of dough.

2. Set the dough on a piece of plastic wrap, and roll it into a neat log. Refrigerate for 45 minutes.

3. Make the vanilla cream: Pour the milk into a medium saucepan. Use a paring knife to split open the vanilla bean lengthwise. Scrape out the seeds with the tip of the knife, and add them to the saucepan along with the pod. Bring the milk with the vanilla to a boil.

4. While the milk is heating, add the egg yolks, brown sugar, and cornstarch to a large heatproof mixing bowl, and whisk vigorously until the mixture turns white. Set aside.

5. Remove the vanilla pod from the boiling milk, and then pour the milk over the eggs and sugar while whis king. When you have a smooth, even mixture, pour the contents of the bowl back into the saucepan. Bring to a simmer, stirring continuously.

VANILLA CREAM

2 cups milk

1 vanilla bean

2 egg yolks

¼ cup brown sugar or granulated sugar

1 teaspoon cornstarch

6. Continue to stir for another 2 minutes, and then pour the cream into 4 bowls. Cover tightly with plastic wrap, and set aside.

7. Preheat the oven to 350°F. Take the dough out of the refrigerator, and remove the plastic wrap. Slice the dough into ¼-inch rounds, and arrange them on a baking sheet lined with parchment paper. Bake for 10 minutes.

8. Remove the cookies from the oven, and transfer immediately to a wire rack.

To plate:
Serve each of your guests a bowl of cream and a few cookies. This dessert can be enjoyed warm, hot, or cold.

Note:
Don't throw out the vanilla pod after you remove it from the boiling milk! Wipe it off with paper towels, and place it in the oven at 195°F for 2 hours to dry it. Then run the dry pod through a food processor or place it in a container of granulated sugar to make homemade vanilla sugar!

LUCKY CAT CAFÉ NEKO MUFFINS

BLACKBERRY MATCHA MUFFINS

DIFFICULTY:
PREP TIME: 20 minutes
COOK TIME: 20 minutes

INGREDIENTS

YIELD: 10 MUFFINS

1 carton blackberries,
about 6 ounces

⅔ cup milk

⅓ cup plus 1 tablespoon butter,
plus more for greasing,
if needed

1 teaspoon culinary
matcha powder

1 egg

¾ cup sugar

1¼ cups flour

2 teaspoons baking powder

Salt

EQUIPMENT

Muffin pan (greased or with
paper muffin liners)

Aunt Cass's wings are spicy enough to numb lips, but her muffins bring comfort to those she loves. Fresh blackberries unite with ground matcha for a delicious, sustaining breakfast for even the busiest of kids.

1. Coarsely chop the blackberries. You want to end up with pieces, not a purée.

2. Combine the milk, butter, and matcha powder in a medium saucepan. Warm over medium heat until the butter is completely melted. Remove the saucepan from heat.

3. Break the egg into a large mixing bowl, and add the sugar. Whisk vigorously until frothy.

4. In a separate medium mixing bowl, combine the flour, baking powder, and a pinch of salt; then add the mixture to the eggs and sugar. Add the matcha-infused milk, and stir until the batter is smooth and even. Add the chopped blackberries, and stir again.

5. Divide the batter among 10 lined or greased muffin tins, and bake for 20 minutes. Serve the muffins warm or at room temperature.

MARIGOLD BRIDGE PAN DE MUERTO

SWEET BUNS WITH ORANGE BLOSSOM WATER

DIFFICULTY: ✿
PREP TIME: 25 minutes
RESTING TIME: 1½ hours
COOK TIME: 40 minutes

INGREDIENTS

YIELD: 4 BUNS

2 teaspoons whole milk,
at room temperature

5 teaspoons active dry yeast

3 eggs

4 egg yolks, divided

¾ cup plus 2 tablespoons
cold butter

1 orange

2⅔ cups cake flour,
plus more for dusting

1 teaspoon salt

2½ tablespoons sugar

2 tablespoons honey

3½ tablespoons
orange blossom water

Granulated or powdered sugar,
for dusting

EQUIPMENT

Stand mixer with
dough hook

Pastry brush

Sharing traditional foods is a way for Miguel and his family to connect with loved ones. This classic pan de muerto recipe creates a sweet crusted bread finished with a dusting of sugar, to glaze the outside right before serving.

1. Pour the milk into a small bowl, and stir in the yeast. Set aside for 5 minutes, to activate.

2. In a separate medium mixing bowl, lightly beat the whole eggs and 2 of the egg yolks; set aside. Cut the butter into small cubes. Zest the orange, and cut the fruit into supremes. Cut each supreme into 4 small pieces.

3. Attach a dough hook to your stand mixer, and add the cake flour to the mixer bowl. Add the salt, sugar, honey, orange blossom water, beaten eggs, and activated yeast and milk, along with the orange zest and pieces. Knead on medium for 2 minutes and then at a higher setting for another 5 minutes until the dough detaches from the sides of the bowl and appears almost even.

4. While continuing to knead, add in the cubed butter. After 2 minutes, the butter should be thoroughly mixed in and the ball of dough should be smooth. Cover with a damp cloth, and set aside for 1 hour.

5. When the dough has finished resting, dust your work surface with flour. Turn out the dough, and punch it down with your fist. Briefly knead the dough, to form it into a nice ball, and then divide it into 5 equal pieces.

6. Roll 4 of the dough pieces in your hands, to form round balls. Cut the final piece into 8 smaller pieces, and roll them into logs. Press 2 dough logs onto the surface of each dough ball in a cross shape. Place the resulting buns on a baking sheet lined with parchment paper. Set aside under a damp cloth for 30 minutes.

7. Preheat the oven to 350°F. In a bowl, beat the 2 remaining egg yolks. Use a pastry brush to brush the yolks over the buns, and then bake for 40 minutes.

To plate:
Dust the buns with sugar or powdered sugar while still hot. Let cool briefly before serving.

PENNY'S COOKIES

GINGER COOKIES

DIFFICULTY: 🐭

PREP TIME: 10 minutes

RESTING TIME: 1 hour

COOK TIME: 15 minutes

INGREDIENTS

YIELD: 4 SERVINGS

½ cup brown sugar

2 tablespoons honey

7 tablespoons butter, at room temperature

1 egg

2 cups flour, plus more for dusting

2 teaspoons baking powder

1 teaspoon ground ginger

Salt

1 ounce candied ginger

EQUIPMENT

3-inch cookie cutter (or cup)

In The Rescuers, *it cheers Penny up to give a gingersnap cookie to her feline friend, Rufus. Sharing these sweet and spicy gingersnaps is a perfect way to show someone you appreciate them.*

1. Preheat the oven to 350°F. Add the brown sugar and honey to a large mixing bowl. Add the butter, and mix with a spatula until smooth. Whisk in the egg.

2. In a separate large mixing bowl, combine the flour, baking powder, ground ginger, and a pinch of salt. Chop the candied ginger, and stir it into the dry ingredients. Combine the dry ingredients with the egg-butter–brown sugar mixture. Mix with your hands to form a ball; then wrap the cookie dough in plastic wrap, and refrigerate for 1 hour.

3. When the dough has chilled, dust your work surface with flour, and roll out the dough to about ¼ inch thick. Use a round cookie cutter or cup to cut out your cookies, and arrange them on a baking sheet lined with parchment paper.

4. Bake for 12 to 15 minutes, and then remove the cookies to a wire rack.

Note:
You can enjoy these cookies right away or keep them in an airtight container for several days.

PANCAKE BREAKFAST

HOMEMADE VANILLA PANCAKES

DIFFICULTY:

PREP TIME: 15 minutes

COOK TIME: 5 minutes,
plus 1½ minutes per pancake

INGREDIENTS

YIELD: 4 SERVINGS

1½ cups milk

5¼ tablespoons butter

3 eggs

¾ cup sugar

1 teaspoon vanilla extract

2½ cups flour

4 teaspoons baking powder

Salt

Butter or vegetable oil,
for frying

Honey or maple syrup,
for serving

In one of the many adventures with Donald, Chip, and Dale, the three fight over pancakes. There's no need to fight now, though! There's enough for everyone with this recipe for vanilla pancakes, hot off the pan.

1. Make the pancake batter: Pour the milk into a medium saucepan, add the butter, and warm over medium heat until the butter is completely melted. Set aside.

2. Break the eggs into a large mixing bowl. Add the sugar and vanilla extract. Whisk vigorously until the eggs are frothy and lighter in color.

3. In a separate large mixing bowl, combine the flour, baking powder, and a pinch of salt; then add it to the egg-sugar mixture. Stir to form a doughlike mixture. Gradually pour in the warm milk and butter while stirring—this will result in a nice, smooth pancake batter with no lumps.

4. Heat a small frying pan over medium heat with a pat of butter or a little vegetable oil. When the pan is smoking hot, pour in 1 ladleful of batter, and swirl to coat the pan. Cook briefly, flipping the pancake when small bubbles appear and remain all over the surface. Repeat until you have used up all the batter.

To plate:
Serve the pancakes in short stacks—3 pancakes per person—with honey or maple syrup.

ADVENTURE IS OUT THERE ICE CREAM

VANILLA ALMOND AND CHOCOLATE HAZELNUT NICE CREAM

DIFFICULTY:
PREP TIME: 10 minutes
RESTING TIME: 12 hours

INGREDIENTS

YIELD: 4 SERVINGS

VANILLA ALMOND NICE CREAM

2 bananas

3 ounces almond cream (see page 28)

1 tablespoon coconut oil

1 teaspoon honey

2 tablespoons vanilla extract

4 waffle cones

CHOCOLATE HAZELNUT NICE CREAM

2 bananas

1 teaspoon dark cocoa powder

3 tablespoons chocolate hazelnut butter

1 teaspoon coconut oil

4 waffle cones

EQUIPMENT

Blender

After an adventure beyond imagination, Carl and Russell enjoy a quiet moment, watching the cars pass while they eat ice cream on the curb. Mix up these two delicious flavors for your own sweet and nutty pairing.

1. The day before, peel the 4 bananas and cut them into chunks. Put them in a freezer bag, and leave them in the freezer overnight.

2. Make the vanilla almond nice cream: Add 2 frozen bananas and the almond cream, coconut oil, honey, and vanilla extract to a blender. Blend on high for 2 to 3 minutes. Use a silicone spatula to scrape the nice cream out of the blender into a medium serving bowl.

3. Make the chocolate hazelnut nice cream: Add 2 frozen bananas and the cocoa powder, chocolate hazelnut butter, and coconut oil to the blender. Blend on high for 2 to 3 minutes. Use a silicone spatula to scrape the nice cream out of the blender into a medium serving bowl.

4. Use an ice cream scoop or a soup spoon to form scoops of nice cream, and place them in the 4 cones.

5. Serve right away!

PORTOROSSO CANNOLI

RICOTTA AND PISTACHIO CANNOLI

DIFFICULTY: 🌿🌿
PREP TIME: 20 minutes
COOK TIME: 7 to 8 minutes

INGREDIENTS

YIELD: 6 SERVINGS

CANNOLI
¼ cup butter
2 egg whites
Salt
¾ cup powdered sugar
½ cup flour
1 vanilla bean

RICOTTA CREAM
1¼ cups ricotta cheese
⅓ cup powdered sugar
2 tablespoons candied cherries
⅔ cup crushed pistachios, for garnish

EQUIPMENT
Hand mixer or whisk
Piping bag
6 stainless-steel cannoli tubes
Skimmer

Giulia and her father welcome Luca and Alberto into their home by sharing their delicious Italian seaside cuisine. Cannoli are rich traditional pastries that epitomize the sweetness and generosity of Italian culture. With their cherry-cheese filling, crunchy exterior, and pistachio-dotted finish, these Portorosso Cannoli are irresistible!

1. Make the cannoli shell dough: In a small saucepan, melt the butter over low heat, and clarify it: Use a small skimmer to remove the foamy milk solids from the top, leaving behind a clear, golden liquid. Remove from heat, and let cool slightly.

2. Add the egg whites and a pinch of salt to a large mixing bowl. Use a whisk or a hand mixer to beat the egg whites until they form stiff peaks, gradually adding in the powdered sugar as you go. When the egg mixture has stiffened, gradually stir in the flour. Slowly add the melted butter by pouring it down the side of the mixing bowl. Finally, use the tip of a knife to scrape the seeds from the vanilla bean, and fold them gently into the cannoli shell dough. Set the dough aside.

3. Preheat the oven to 350°F. Line a baking sheet with parchment paper. Use a soup spoon to scoop small mounds of cannoli dough onto the parchment paper. Flatten the mounds into circles about 3 to 4 inches in diameter. Bake for 7 to 8 minutes.

4. Remove the baking sheet from the oven. Carefully unstick each dough round (which should be cooked but still flexible), and roll around one of the cannoli tubes. Leave the dough around the tube briefly to set, and then gently slide it off. Cover the cannoli shells with a clean cloth until you are ready to fill them.

5. Make the ricotta cream: Place the ricotta in a large mixing bowl, and add the powdered sugar. Whisk vigorously until smooth and luscious; set aside. Coarsely chop the candied cherries, and stir them into the whipped ricotta.

6. Transfer the ricotta-cherry filling to a piping bag, and fill the cannoli shells.

7. Cover the ends of your cannoli with crushed pistachios by pressing the nuts into the surface of the ricotta. *Buon appetito!*

MAMA MADRIGAL'S BUÑUELOS

SWEET CHEESE FRITTERS

DIFFICULTY:
PREP TIME: 20 minutes
COOK TIME: 10 minutes

INGREDIENTS

YIELD: 4 SERVINGS

7 ounces feta cheese
1 whole egg plus 1 yolk
1½ tablespoons butter
1 cup cassava flour
Scant ½ cup cornstarch
¼ cup sugar
1 teaspoon salt
1 teaspoon baking powder
3 tablespoons milk
8 cups vegetable oil, for frying
Melted chocolate
Honey

EQUIPMENT

Dutch oven or deep fryer
Cooking thermometer
Skimmer or strainer,
for deep frying

Buñuelos are delicious cheese fritters that are traditionally served around Christmas in Colombia. Julieta Madrigal's buñuelos are soft and delicious. They taste of happiness, and just a bite of one can make anyone smile!

1. Drain and crumble the feta; set aside. In a medium mixing bowl, beat the egg and egg yolk; set aside. Cut the butter into pieces; set aside.

2. Stir together the feta, cassava flour, cornstarch, sugar, salt, and baking powder in a large mixing bowl. Add the butter, milk, and beaten eggs. Knead by hand for 5 minutes until the dough is smooth and even.

3. Pull off a piece of dough about the size of a golf ball, and roll it in your hands to form a round ball. Repeat until you have used up all the dough.

4. In a large Dutch oven or deep fryer, heat the oil to 340°F. Meanwhile, set out several paper towels on a plate.

5. When the oil is hot, drop in the dough balls; fry them for about 1½ minutes each until they are golden brown and float to the surface of the oil.

6. Use a skimmer or a spider strainer to remove the buñuelos from the oil and transfer them to the paper towels. Serve hot, with melted chocolate or honey!

SWEET BAO

DUMPLINGS WITH RED BEAN PASTE

DIFFICULTY:
PREP TIME: 15 minutes
RESTING TIME: 15 minutes
COOK TIME: 10 minutes

INGREDIENTS

YIELD: 10 BAO

2 cups dumpling flour,
plus more for dusting

2 cups plus 2 tablespoons water,
at room temperature

7 ounces anko paste,
storebought or homemade
(see Tip on page 127)

EQUIPMENT

Steamer basket

In a Toronto kitchen, a caring wife creates a delicious bao. Surprise! The bao comes to life! As that little bao grows up, life's lessons come to both mother and child. Follow this recipe to create your very own sweet, pillowy-soft bao to savor with your loved ones.

1. Make the dumpling dough: Pour the flour into a large mixing bowl, and form a well in the center. Pour the water into the well. Use your fingertips to bring the flour into the water, and then knead with your entire hands for 3 minutes to form a dough. Dust your work surface with flour, transfer your dough to your work surface, and continue to knead for another 10 minutes until you have a smooth ball of dough.

2. Cover, and set aside for 15 minutes.

3. Dust your work surface with flour again, and set the dough on it. Form the dough into a thick log, and cut it into 10 equal pieces. Roll out each piece into a disc about 4 inches in diameter.

4. Take 1 disc in the palm of your hand, and place 1 teaspoon of anko paste in the center. Fold the edges up over the filling, and pinch so that the wrapper flares out at the top (*see Step by Step on page 74 for instructions on folding bao*). Repeat for each disc of dough. Your sweet bao are almost ready.

5. Place the bao in a steamer basket on a sheet of parchment paper. Bring the water under the steamer basket to a boil, and steam the buns for 10 minutes. Keep the water boiling over medium heat—the steam should not be too intense. When the bao are cooked, remove them from the steamer basket. Serve right away.

STEP BY STEP

FOLDING BAO

INGREDIENTS

2 cups dumpling flour, plus more for dusting

2 cups plus 2 tablespoons water, at room temperature

7 ounces anko paste, storebought or homemade (see Tip on page 127)

1. Add the flour to a large mixing bowl, and form a well in the center. Pour the water into the well.

2. Use your fingertips to bring the flour into the water, and then knead with your entire hands for 3 minutes to form a dough.

3. Dust your work surface with flour, place your dough on your work surface, and continue to knead for another 10 minutes until you have a smooth ball of dough. Cover, and set aside for 15 minutes.

4. Dust your work surface with flour, and turn out the dough onto it. Form the dough into a thick log.

5. Cut the log into 10 equal pieces.

6. Roll out each piece into a disc about 4 inches in diameter (you can use a 4-inch round cookie cutter to make perfectly round discs).

7. Take 1 disc in the palm of your hand, and place 1 teaspoon of anko paste in the center.

8–9. Fold the edges up over the filling, and pinch so that the wrapper flares out at the top.

10. Repeat for each disc of dough. Your sweet bao are almost ready. As you fold each one, place it in a steamer basket lined with parchment paper.

ONE EXTRATERRESTRIAL BITE CAKE

BLACK FOREST CAKE

Stitch doesn't take his time and savor his food—he gulps it in one go! This delicious chocolate cake has candied cherries between the layers and is frosted with a thick coating of whipped cream. You might be tempted to eat it all up before anyone else has a chance to try it!

DIFFICULTY: ❀
PREP TIME: 20 minutes
COOK TIME: 30 minutes

INGREDIENTS

YIELD: 6 SERVINGS

CHOCOLATE CAKE LAYERS

1¾ tablespoons butter, plus more for greasing

4 eggs

Salt

½ cup plus 2 tablespoons sugar

⅔ cup flour

3¼ tablespoons dark cocoa powder

WHIPPED CREAM

3 cups heavy whipping cream, very cold

⅔ cup powdered sugar

½ cup plus 1 tablespoon sweet syrup, such as cherry syrup, divided

20 candied cherries

EQUIPMENT

10-inch springform pan

Hand mixer or whisk

Pastry brush

1. Make the cake: Preheat the oven to 350°F. Grease the springform pan with butter. In a medium saucepan, melt the butter over low heat, and set aside to cool. Break the eggs, and separate the yolks and whites into 2 large mixing bowls.

2. Add a pinch of salt to the mixing bowl with the egg whites. Beat the egg whites until they form stiff peaks; set aside. Add the sugar to the bowl with the egg yolks. Whisk vigorously until the mixture is thick and frothy; set aside. Mix together the flour and cocoa powder in another large mixing bowl, and then stir in the egg yolk–sugar mixture. Use a silicone spatula to fold in the stiff egg whites little by little, to obtain a smooth, creamy texture. Finally, stir in the melted and cooled butter.

3. Your cake batter is ready! Pour it into the springform pan, and bake for 30 minutes. Then remove the cake from the pan, and set it on a wire rack, allowing it to cool to room temperature while remaining soft.

4. Make the whipped cream: Pour the whipping cream into a large chilled mixing bowl, and whisk vigorously until it starts to become dense and firm. Add the powdered sugar, and continue to whisk until you have a nice, firm whipped cream. Set aside in the refrigerator.

5. Begin assembling your black forest cake: Use a knife to carefully cut the cake into 2 layers of equal thickness (*see Step by Step on page 42*). Place one layer on the serving plate, and use a pastry brush to moisten the cake with half the syrup. Generously sprinkle the bottom cake layer with half the candied cherries, and then cover them with a thick layer of whipped cream. Set the second layer on top. Use a brush to moisten this layer with the remaining syrup. Coat the cake with the remaining whipped cream, and arrange the remaining cherries on top. Cut the cake into generous slices to share, and enjoy!

IT'S JAMMED! EXPLOSIVE PB&J

BUTTERED HONEYED PEANUT BUTTER AND JELLY SANDWICH

DIFFICULTY: ⚙ ⚙
PREP TIME: 10 minutes
COOK TIME: 4 minutes

INGREDIENTS

YIELD: 4 SERVINGS

HOMEMADE HONEY PEANUT BUTTER

⅔ cup plus 3 tablespoons organic peanuts, divided

1 tablespoon neutral vegetable oil

1 tablespoon honey

8 thick slices brioche (or sandwich) bread

⅓ cup salted butter

4 tablespoons blueberry or strawberry jam

EQUIPMENT

Blender

Lewis knows it just takes imagination and a little science to make the world a better place. There's always room for improvement! Try out this buttery honey peanut butter sandwich for a quick and delicious take on the standard. Don't worry—in this case, the explosion just refers to the flavor!

1. Make the honey peanut butter: Heat a medium frying pan over medium heat, and add ⅔ cup shelled peanuts. Roast for 1 to 2 minutes, and then transfer to a blender. Blend the peanuts in several phases: Blend constantly for 30 seconds to reduce them to a powder, and then continue to pulse for another 2 to 4 minutes. You'll see their consistency transform from large crushed pieces to powder; then to a thick, gritty paste; and finally to a nearly smooth butter. Crush the remaining 3 tablespoons peanuts, and stir them in, along with the oil and honey, using a wooden spoon. You can store your homemade peanut butter for several days in an airtight jar.

2. Preheat the oven to 400°F. Make the sandwiches: Spread the slices of bread with butter, and arrange them on a baking sheet lined with parchment paper. Bake for 3 to 4 minutes, flipping halfway through so that they come out perfectly browned and toasted.

3. Take the bread out of the oven. Spread a thick layer of jam on 4 pieces of bread. Spread an even layer of peanut butter on the other 4 pieces of bread. Piece the sandwiches together, and enjoy right away. And don't forget to share with your roommate!

REGULAR OLE LIVING PECAN PIE

DINER-STYLE PECAN PIE

DIFFICULTY:
PREP TIME: 10 minutes
COOK TIME: 40 minutes

INGREDIENTS

YIELD: 4 SERVINGS

¼ cup butter, plus more
for greasing

8½ ounces shortbread crust
(see Tip on page 110)

2 cups raw pecans

⅓ cup brown sugar

4 eggs

⅔ cup maple syrup

4 teaspoons bourbon
vanilla extract

EQUIPMENT

Pie plate
Pie weights (or dry beans)

Listening to music, riding a bike in summer, feeling the ocean lap upon your toes, and eating pecan pie at a diner on a snowy night: Joe Gardner finally realizes that these everyday joys make life worth living. Reminisce on the finer joys of a life well lived while you bake and enjoy this seasonal standard.

1. Preheat the oven to 350°F. Grease the pie plate, and line it with the shortbread crust: Place the pie crust into the pie plate, and use your fingertips to press it firmly against the sides. Crimp the edges. Prick the crust with a fork.

2. Cover the crust with parchment paper, and weight it down with pie weights (or dry beans) to prevent it from puffing up during baking (*see Step by Step on page 82*). Bake for 10 minutes; then remove from the oven, remove the pie weights (or dry beans), and set aside.

3. Make the pecan filling: Coarsely chop 1½ cups pecans. In a large mixing bowl, cream together the brown sugar and butter with a silicone spatula. When the mixture is smooth, whisk in the eggs one by one. Stir in the maple syrup and vanilla extract, and then add the chopped pecans.

4. Stir well. Pour the mixture into the blind baked pie crust. Arrange the remaining whole pecans over the top of the pie, and bake for 30 minutes. Serve warm or cold.

STEP BY STEP

BLIND BAKING
A CRUST

INGREDIENTS

8½ ounces shortbread crust
(see Tip on page 110)

1. Preheat the oven to 350°F. Grease the pie plate, and dust with flour.

   Roll out the shortbread crust, and press it into the pie plate. Use your fingertips to press it firmly against the sides, taking care not to tear it.

2. Remove any excess dough by running a knife around the top edge (if you have enough left, you can make another pie crust. You can also use a cookie cutter to make shortbread cookies from the remnant).

3. Prick the crust with a fork.

4. Lay a piece of parchment paper over the crust. Weight it down with a thick layer of pie weights (or dry beans).

5. Bake for 10 minutes, and then remove the pie plate from the oven.

6. Let the blind baked crust cool slightly. Remove the pie weights (or dry beans). Your crust is ready to be filled (with ▶ chocolate ganache, pastry cream and fruit, or other filling).

FANTASY
WORLDS

PAWPSICLES

STRAWBERRY VERBENA ICE POPS

Nick and Finnick can make a lot of pawpsicles—and a lot of money!—from one melted jumbo pop. Here's a paw-shape popsicle recipe that's perfectly legal and less risky to make, but equally delicious and refreshing.

DIFFICULTY:

PREP TIME: 15 minutes

COOK TIME: 30 minutes

RESTING TIME: 6 hours

INGREDIENTS

YIELD: 10 ICE POPS

STRAWBERRY VERBENA SYRUP

18 ounces organic strawberries

Handful of verbena leaves

1¾ cups sugar

1 cup water

4 cups mineral water

EQUIPMENT

Paw-shape ice pop mold

1. Hull and chop the strawberries. Add them to a large saucepan, along with the verbena leaves, sugar, and water. (For plain strawberry syrup, just skip the verbena.)

2. Cook over medium heat for 30 minutes, stirring regularly. Mash the strawberries, to release their juices. Strain the contents of the saucepan into a small saucepan, to separate the liquid syrup from the stewed strawberries. (But don't let the cooked strawberries and verbena go to waste—you can blend them into a strawberry compote!)

3. Reduce the syrup for 2 to 4 minutes over medium heat until it is as syrupy as possible. Your strawberry verbena syrup is ready!

4. Dilute the syrup with mineral water, according to your taste. Pour the flavored water into ice pop molds, and freeze for 6 hours before serving.

Note:
You can make this very simple recipe even simpler by using storebought fruit syrup. However, if you take the opportunity to practice making your own fruit syrup, the results will be even better!

CARROT POPS

CANDIED CARROT LOLLIPOPS

DIFFICULTY:

PREP TIME: 10 minutes

COOK TIME: 30 to 40 minutes

RESTING TIME: 1 hour

INGREDIENTS

YIELD: 4 SERVINGS

1 pound butter

1 cup sugar

2 tablespoons salt

2-inch piece of fresh ginger

4 large carrots or 8 small carrots

4 speculoos cookies

4 teaspoons honey

EQUIPMENT

4 or 8 wooden skewers

According to Judy Hopps's parents, there's no better way to improve the world than to become a carrot farmer, a noble profession they envision for Judy and all her 275 brothers and sisters. Judy has a different idea for her future, of course, but she still enjoys carrots—she's a bunny, after all! This sweet carrot treat will put a hop and a skip in your step.

1. Fill a large Dutch oven with water. Cut the butter into pieces, and add it to the water, along with the sugar and salt. Smash the ginger with the flat side of a knife blade, and drop it into the Dutch oven. Bring the contents of the Dutch oven to a gentle boil.

2. Meanwhile, peel the carrots, and drop them in as well. Maintain a gentle boil, to poach the carrots for 30 to 40 minutes.

3. Drain the carrots, set them aside, and let them cool to room temperature. When they have cooled, refrigerate the carrots for 1 hour.

To plate:
Crush the speculoos cookies. Skewer the carrots from their ends. Drizzle each carrot with honey, and sprinkle with crushed cookies. Enjoy!

RANDALL'S BE MY PAL CUPCAKES

CHOCOLATE CUPCAKES WITH VANILLA FROSTING

DIFFICULTY:
PREP TIME: 30 minutes
COOK TIME: 15 minutes

INGREDIENTS

YIELD: 4 SERVINGS
(8 CUPCAKES)

CUPCAKES

½ cup sugar

4 eggs

¾ cup flour

2 teaspoons baking powder

2 tablespoons dark cocoa powder

½ cup butter

FROSTING

1 cup heavy whipping cream, very cold

2 tablespoons powdered sugar

2 tablespoons mascarpone

4 teaspoons vanilla extract

EQUIPMENT

Red cake writing gel

Cupcake pan with paper or silicone liners

Piping bag

Hand mixer or stand mixer

Meeting new people in college can be difficult, even for monsters. And Randall doesn't want to study. Instead, he wants to go to parties and make friends—that's why he makes these scrumptious chocolate cupcakes with a special request.

1. Preheat the oven to 350°F. Make the cupcake batter: Add the sugar and eggs to a large mixing bowl. Whisk until the mixture is smooth and even. Pour in the flour, baking powder, and dark cocoa powder. Thoroughly whisk together all the ingredients, to combine.

2. Melt the butter in a microwave or small saucepan over low heat. Then add it into the rest of the ingredients, one third at a time, stirring to incorporate each addition.

3. Pour the batter into the lined cupcake pan, and bake for 15 minutes.

4. Remove the cupcakes from the oven, and let cool to room temperature on a wire rack.

5. While the cupcakes are baking, make the frosting: Pour the whipping cream into a mixing bowl, and whisk vigorously either manually or with a hand mixer or stand mixer. When the cream starts to thicken, add the powdered sugar. Continue to whisk until you have a firm whipped cream. Stir in the mascarpone and vanilla extract. Transfer the frosting to a piping bag.

To assemble:
Pipe a layer of frosting onto each cupcake. Use an angled spatula or a soup spoon to smooth out the frosting. Then use the red gel to write one letter per cupcake, spelling out BE MY PAL on 7 of the cupcakes. Enjoy!

STEP BY STEP

PIPING FROSTING

1. Make the vanilla whipped cream: Pour the whipping cream into the chilled bowl of a stand mixer, and whisk vigorously. When the cream starts to thicken, add the powdered sugar. Continue to whisk until you have a firm whipped cream. Stir in the mascarpone and vanilla extract. Place your selected tip into the bottom of the piping bag, and use your thumb to gently tuck part of the bag into the tip, blocking the hole. This prevents your frosting from leaking out as you fill the bag.

2. Open the piping bag, folding it down over itself.

3. Place one hand under the folded bag, and use a spatula to fill the bag with frosting.

4. Press the frosting down into the bag, using the spatula or a bowl scraper to remove any air pockets. Untuck the bag from the tip, to allow the frosting to flow out.

5. Fold down the bag, to push the frosting toward the tip. Roll the top of the bag around your thumb, and pipe frosting onto your cake or cupcakes. The results will look different, depending on the tip you choose. You can pipe in a swirl pattern (photo 5) or make frosting stars all over the top (opposite photo).

Note:
Try adding a few drops of food coloring to your frosting, for colorful cupcakes.

INGREDIENTS

1 cup heavy whipping cream, very cold

2 tablespoons powdered sugar

2 tablespoons mascarpone

4 teaspoons vanilla extract

1 cake or batch of cupcakes, cooled

EQUIPMENT

Stand mixer

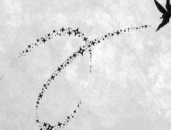

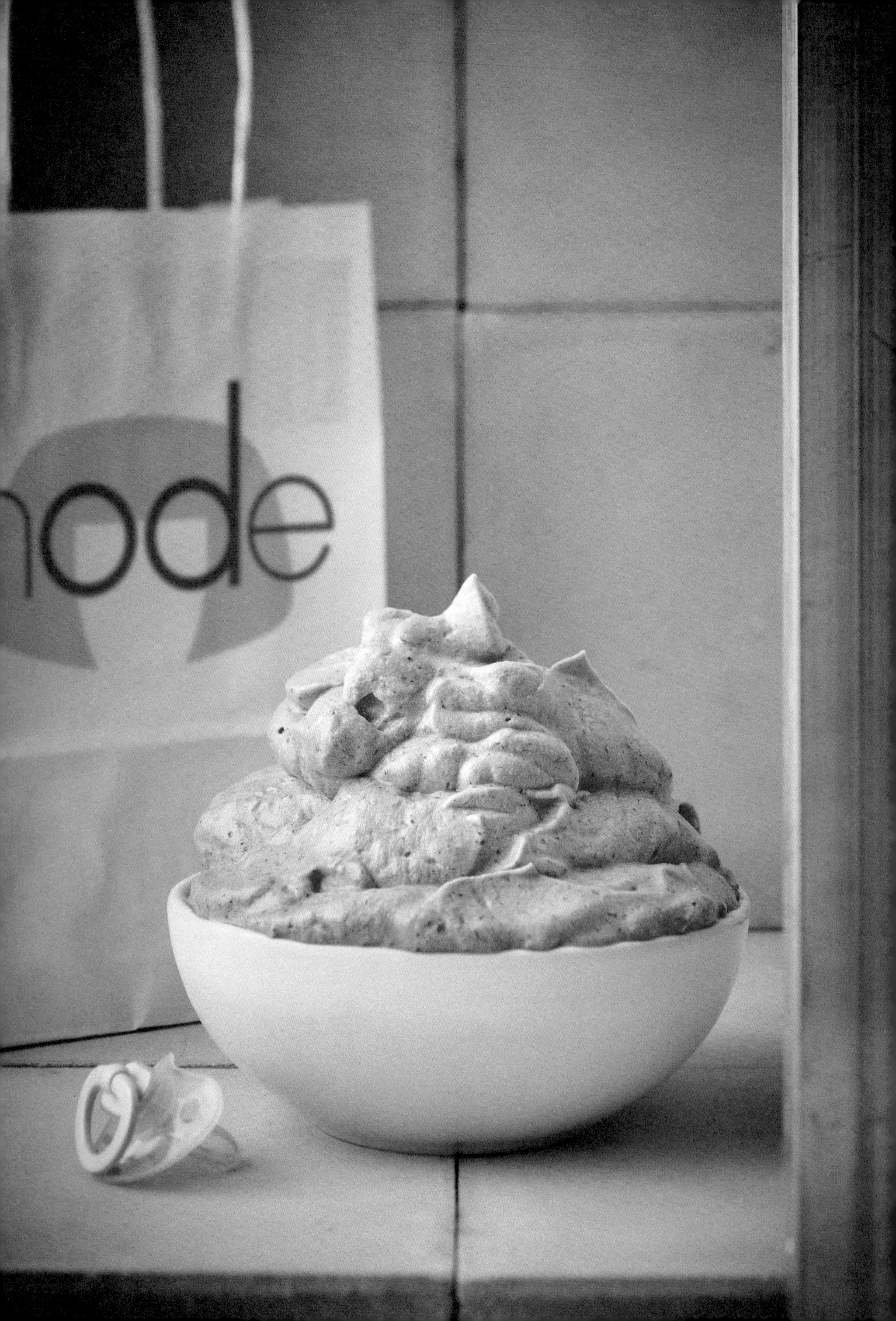
node

MOUSSE FOR JACK-JACK

BLACKBERRY LAVENDER MOUSSE

DIFFICULTY:
PREP TIME: 10 minutes
RESTING TIME: 1 hour

INGREDIENTS

YIELD: 4 SERVINGS

BLACKBERRY COULIS

1⅔ cups blackberries

3 pasteurized egg whites
3 tablespoons granulated sugar

**LAVENDER
WHIPPED CREAM**

⅔ cup heavy whipping cream,
very cold
2 tablespoons powdered sugar
4 teaspoons lavender syrup

EQUIPMENT

Blender
Strainer
Hand mixer

When Jack-Jack disappears to the other dimension, he can still hear his dad calling, and he'll listen—that is, if his dad is offering Jack-Jack a sweet treat. Summon your own inner child with this sugary super-whipped mousse.

1. Make the blackberry coulis: Put the blackberries in the blender. Blend for 2 minutes. Then strain and keep the liquid: a syrupy, seed-free coulis. Set aside.

2. Add the egg whites to a large mixing bowl, and beat until they form peaks. Whisk in the granulated sugar, to stiffen the egg whites. Set aside.

3. Make the lavender whipped cream: Pour the whipping cream into a large chilled mixing bowl, and whisk vigorously until it increases in volume. When the whipped cream starts to firm up, add the powdered sugar. Whisk for another 2 minutes, and then add the lavender syrup.

4. Use a silicone spatula to fold the fluffy egg whites into the lavender whipped cream. Fold very carefully, to avoid deflating them. Gently stir in the blackberry coulis.

5. Transfer the mousse to a large serving bowl, cover the surface with plastic wrap, and refrigerate for at least 1 hour before serving.

EVERYDAY WAFFLES FOR NOT-SO-EVERYDAY KIDS

WAFFLES WITH SALTED BUTTER AND MAPLE SYRUP

DIFFICULTY:
PREP TIME: 15 minutes
COOK TIME: 10 to 15 minutes

INGREDIENTS

YIELD: 4 SERVINGS

2 cups flour, sifted
2 teaspoons baking powder
2 pinches of salt
2 eggs
⅓ cup sugar
2 cups milk
4 teaspoons vanilla extract
5½ tablespoons melted butter
Neutral vegetable oil,
for greasing
Powdered sugar, for serving
Salted butter, for serving
Caramel, for serving
Maple syrup, for serving

EQUIPMENT

Hand mixer
Waffle maker (or waffle iron)

Teenagers are teenagers—even if they're also superheroes. Violet decides to show some teen spirit when her dad is cooking up some waffles. She storms in, says her piece, and then storms back out. Jack-Jack, Dash, and Bob simply relax and eat their waffles, just like any everyday family.

1. In a large mixing bowl, stir together the flour, baking powder, and 1 pinch of salt. Crack the eggs, and separate the whites from the yolks in 2 separate large mixing bowls. Add the second pinch of salt to the egg whites, and beat until stiff. Set aside.

2. Add the sugar to the egg yolks, and whisk vigorously until the mixture is frothy and lighter in color. Stir in the milk, vanilla extract, and melted butter. Whisk in the dry ingredient mixture until the batter is smooth, with no lumps. Gently stir in the egg whites.

3. Cook the waffles: Grease the waffle maker with the neutral oil, and preheat it; then pour in the batter. Cook for 3 to 5 minutes, depending on your preferred texture.

To plate:
Serve the waffles piping hot, dusted with powdered sugar. Top each with a generous pat of salted butter, and drizzle with caramel or maple syrup!

HERCULES FAN COLA

HOMEMADE COLA WITH GREEK CITRUS

DIFFICULTY:
PREP TIME: 10 minutes
COOK TIME: 10 minutes

INGREDIENTS

YIELD: 4 SERVINGS

CITRUS SYRUP

2 organic Valencia oranges

1 vanilla bean

½-inch piece of fresh ginger

1½ cups brown sugar

1¼ to 1½ cups water

3½ tablespoons
pomegranate juice

2 star anise

1 stick cinnamon

A few mint leaves

1 liter lemon-lime soda, tonic
water, or sparkling water

Hercules is so popular that Hercules-branded merch is everywhere. Pain and Panic give in to the temptation to join the trend, but Hades is outraged when he catches Panic sipping a Hercules drink. Quench your thirst with tastes of the Greek gods with this citrus-mint soda. Don't worry—Hades won't come after you for it.

1. Peel and press the oranges. Reserve the juice, and set aside the peels. Use a paring knife to split the vanilla bean in half lengthwise. Scrape out the seeds, reserving them, and cut the empty pod into small pieces. Smash the ginger.

2. Add the brown sugar, water, orange juice, and pomegranate juice to a medium saucepan. Mix well, and warm over medium heat for 5 minutes to fully dissolve the sugar.

3. Add the orange peels, star anise, cinnamon, vanilla seeds and pod pieces, ginger, and mint. Bring to a simmer, and reduce to a syrupy texture with concentrated flavors.

4. Strain and keep the liquid. You can keep this full-strength citrus-mint syrup in an airtight bottle in the refrigerator for several weeks.

To serve:
Add 1 or 2 tablespoons syrup to a glass, and dilute with cold lemon-lime soda or sparkling water. Enjoy immediately!

KUMANDRA ICED TEA

ICED TEA WITH JASMINE, CHILE PEPPERS, LEMONGRASS, AND PALM SUGAR

DIFFICULTY: ❋
PREP TIME: 5 minutes
COOK TIME: 5 minutes
RESTING TIME: 30 minutes

INGREDIENTS

YIELD: 4 CUPS ICED TEA

1 lemongrass stalk
⅓ cup palm sugar
2 small chile peppers
4½ cups mineral water
2½ tablespoons loose black tea
2 dried hibiscus flowers
Handful of jasmine flowers
Crushed ice, for serving
Cane syrup or honey, for serving

EQUIPMENT

Cooking thermometer

When Raya, Sisu, Tong, Boun, and Little Noi sit down to share a meal, they also share their dreams of reuniting with friends and family. This sweet and spicy refreshing drink is perfect for sharing with your own loved ones.

1. Chop the lemongrass into large pieces. Break up the palm sugar. Destem the chile peppers, and use the tip of a paring knife to remove the seeds. Wash your hands after handling the seeds.

2. Pour the mineral water into a large saucepan, and bring it to a simmer (never hotter than 185°F). Drop in the tea, lemongrass, hibiscus flowers, jasmine flowers, palm sugar, and chile peppers. Continue to simmer for 5 minutes, and then remove the saucepan from heat. Cover, and allow the ingredients to steep in the hot water for 30 minutes.

3. Strain the tea, pour it into a bottle, and refrigerate.

To serve:
Serve this Kumandra Iced Tea over crushed ice. You can adjust the sweetness by adding a little cane syrup or honey!

LEGENDARY STICKY RICE

COCONUT STICKY RICE WITH MANGO

DIFFICULTY: ❊
PREP TIME: 15 minutes
RESTING TIME: 3 hours
COOK TIME: 45 minutes

INGREDIENTS

YIELD: 4 SERVINGS

1¼ cups Thai sticky rice

2 very ripe mangoes

2½ cups coconut milk

¼ cup sugar

1 teaspoon salt

2 very ripe bananas

1 organic lime (juice and zest)

¾ cup sliced almonds

EQUIPMENT

4 bamboo steamer baskets

This sweet, hearty dish would fit right in at Boun's Shrimporium. Made with tropical fruits and coconut milk atop sticky rice, it's finished with the bright juice and zest of a fresh lime.

1. Preheat the oven to 400°F. Rinse the sticky rice in 2 or 3 changes of water. Drain the rice, and divide it among 4 small bamboo steamer baskets. Steam for 35 to 40 minutes.

2. Meanwhile, oven-roast the mangoes: Arrange them on a baking sheet lined with parchment paper, and bake for 20 minutes. Set aside.

3. Pour the coconut milk into a medium saucepan, along with the sugar and salt. Bring to a simmer, taking care never to let the coconut milk boil. Set aside.

4. When the rice is finished steaming, transfer it to 4 bowls or soup plates. Pour the sweet coconut milk over the top, and let it absorb for several minutes.

5. Peel the bananas, and mash them with a fork. Peel and slice the mangoes.

To plate:
Garnish each bowl of coconut rice with the mango slices and mashed banana. Drizzle with 1 teaspoon lime juice, and sprinkle with lime zest and sliced almonds. Enjoy!

PIZZA FROM THE GREAT BEYOND

DESSERT PIZZA WITH FRUIT, WHITE CHOCOLATE, AND ALMOND BUTTER

DIFFICULTY: 🍗🍗

PREP TIME: 20 minutes

COOK TIME: 25 minutes

INGREDIENTS

YIELD: 4 SERVINGS

3 ounces white chocolate

3½ tablespoons almond butter

8½ ounces homemade pizza dough (see Tip on page 113)

1 banana

1 kiwi

10 blueberries

EQUIPMENT

Baking stone

Cooking thermometer

Tasting food—New York pizza, no less!—helps 22 understand why people want to live. And after that first bite, 22 can't pass up any chance to partake in the joy of eating. Here's a pizza recipe with a heavenly spin: It's an irresistible dessert pizza!

1. Place a baking stone on the bottom oven rack, and preheat the oven to 425°F. Make the white "sauce": Melt the white chocolate in a double boiler, taking care never to let the temperature exceed 100°F (use a cooking thermometer). Stir in the almond butter with a silicone spatula. Your cream sauce is ready.

2. Roll out the pizza dough on your work surface, and then carefully transfer it to the baking stone to bake for 15 to 20 minutes.

3. Prepare the fruit: Peel and slice the banana and kiwi. Rinse the blueberries, and pat dry.

4. Assemble the pizza: Spread the white chocolate cream over the crust, and top with banana and kiwi slices and blueberries. Enjoy!

ICED ROYAL CROWN CAKE

FLUFFY BUNDT CAKE WITH SEVILLE ORANGE, ORANGE GLAZE,
AND CANDIED GINGER

Surrounded by snow, Olaf dreams of summer—not that he really knows what that means for snowmen like himself! This royal crown cake is frosted to look like it's snow covered, but the cake itself will warm you up with its candied ginger and orange flavors.

DIFFICULTY:
PREP TIME: 15 minutes
COOK TIME: 35 minutes

INGREDIENTS

YIELD: 6 SERVINGS

CAKE

1½ cups flour

2 teaspoons baking powder

Salt

¾ cup butter,
plus more for greasing

4 eggs

½ cup brown sugar

½ cup Seville
orange marmalade

3½ tablespoons whole milk

GLAZE

1 or 2 organic oranges

3 egg whites

2 tablespoons powdered sugar

1½ ounces candied ginger,
for garnish

EQUIPMENT

Bundt pan

1. Preheat the oven to 350°F. Stir together the flour, baking powder, and a pinch of salt in a large mixing bowl. Set aside.

2. In a medium saucepan, melt the butter over low heat; then remove the saucepan from heat.

3. Crack the eggs, and separate the whites from the yolks, putting each in its own large mixing bowl. Add the brown sugar to the bowl with the egg yolks. Whisk vigorously until frothy and thoroughly combined. Whisk in the marmalade, milk, and melted butter. Add the dry ingredients, and stir to combine.

4. Beat the egg whites until they form stiff peaks, taking care not to overmix. Use a silicone spatula to fold the egg whites into the batter delicately, so as not to deflate them.

5. Grease the Bundt pan, pour the batter into it, and then bake for 35 minutes. Turn out the cake onto a wire rack.

6. While the cake is cooking, make the orange glaze: Zest the oranges, and reserve for the garnish. Juice the oranges, and place the juice in a large mixing bowl. Add the egg whites and powdered sugar to the juice. Whisk into a thick icing. Dip the top of the cake into the icing, and then set it right-side up on a serving platter. Sprinkle with orange zest, and garnish with pieces of candied ginger.

TIPS

DOUGHS AND CRUSTS

PIE CRUST

PREP TIME: 10 minutes
RESTING TIME: 30 minutes

INGREDIENTS

1 egg yolk

1 teaspoon salt

3½ tablespoons water

½ cup plus 1 tablespoon butter, at room temperature

2 cups flour

¼ cup sugar

1. Add the egg yolk, salt, and water to a large mixing bowl. Mix, and set aside. Cut the butter into pieces. Sift the flour into a large mixing bowl. Mix in the sugar. Pour the flour-sugar mixture onto your work surface, and form a well in the center.

2. Place the pieces of butter on top of the flour. Pour the egg yolk mixture into the well. Mix the ingredients together, and work the dough briefly but do not knead. When you have a smooth dough, gather it into a ball. Wrap the dough in plastic wrap, and refrigerate for at least 30 minutes.

SHORTBREAD CRUST

PREP TIME: 10 minutes
RESTING TIME: 30 minutes

INGREDIENTS

½ cup plus 1 tablespoon butter, at room temperature

2 cups flour

Scant ½ cup powdered sugar

1 egg yolk

2 tablespoons cold water

Fine salt

1. Cut the butter into pieces. Place the butter in a large mixing bowl, and add the flour. Use your fingertips to rub the butter into the flour until it takes on a sandy consistency. When the butter has been completely incorporated into the flour, add the powdered sugar and egg yolk.

2. Knead with your fingertips; then add the water and a pinch of salt. As soon as the dough becomes smooth, gather it into a ball and wrap it in plastic wrap. Refrigerate for at least 30 minutes.

PUFF PASTRY

PREP TIME
(INCLUDING RESTING TIME):
6 hours or more

INGREDIENTS

1⅔ cups all-purpose flour, plus more for dusting

3½ tablespoons butter, at room temperature, plus ⅔ cup butter, very cold, divided

⅓ cup water

1 teaspoon salt

This recipe requires patience: You won't be able to create thin layers if you skimp on the resting times.

1. Add the flour, butter, water, and salt to a large mixing bowl, and knead to form a smooth ball of dough. Form it into a thick rectangle. Use a paring knife to slash an X into the surface of the dough, and then cover it with plastic wrap. Refrigerate the dough for 30 minutes.

2. Dust your work surface with flour—this will make it easier to handle the dough. Flatten the dough slightly with the palm of your hand; then use a rolling pin to roll it out, leaving the center slightly thicker. Place the cold butter on top of the dough, and fold the sides of the dough up over it. Flip the dough over, and sprinkle with a generous pinch of flour.

3. With the rolling pin, roll out the dough to form a rectangle that is 3 times longer than it is wide. Rotate the dough ¼ turn, and fold the dough in thirds like a letter—first the right side and then the left. Refrigerate the dough for 30 minutes, and then place it back on your work surface in the same orientation as before—that's important!

4. Sprinkle the dough with more flour. Roll it out into a rectangle that is 3 times longer than it is wide. Rotate the dough another ¼ turn, and fold in the sides. Refrigerate for 1 hour. Repeat these steps 4 to 6 times for puff pastry that will really puff!

CHOUX PASTRY

PREP TIME: 15 minutes
RESTING TIME: 15 minutes

INGREDIENTS

5½ tablespoons butter

1 cup water or milk

Salt

1 cup plus 3 tablespoons flour

3 eggs

1. Cut the butter into pieces. Pour the water (or milk) into a large saucepan. Add the butter and a pinch of salt. Warm over medium heat until the liquid boils and the butter has completely melted.

2. Remove the saucepan from heat, and add the flour. Use a spatula to vigorously stir the flour into the liquid until it forms a smooth paste. Return the saucepan to heat, and warm over low heat to dry out the paste. As soon as you see a thin film begin to form on the bottom of the saucepan, remove from heat; transfer the paste to a large heatproof mixing bowl.

3. Add the eggs, one at a time, and continue stirring until the resulting batter forms little peaks when you touch it with your spatula. Transfer to a piping bag, and use it to form cream puffs, éclairs, or gougères.

To make delicious chouquettes, simply add 2 tablespoons powdered sugar to the dough after you have stirred in the eggs. Pipe the sweet choux pastry onto a baking sheet, sprinkle with coarse granulated sugar, and bake for 15 minutes at 400°F.

SWEET ALMOND DOUGH
(based on a recipe by Pierre Hermé)

PREP TIME: 10 minutes
RESTING TIME: 30 minutes

INGREDIENTS

½ cup plus 2 tablespoons butter, at room temperature

⅔ cup powdered sugar

½ teaspoon salt

¼ cup almond flour

1 egg

2 cups all-purpose flour

1. Place the butter in a large mixing bowl. Beat the butter with a silicone spatula until softened. Add the powdered sugar, salt, almond flour, and egg. Thoroughly combine all the ingredients, and then mix in the all-purpose flour. Form the dough into a ball, taking care not to overwork it or knead it too much. When you have a smooth ball of dough, wrap it in plastic wrap and refrigerate for at least 30 minutes.

2. When the dough is very cold, roll it out and line baking rings with circles of dough. Then blind bake the crusts in the rings (*see Step by Step on page 82*). Now they're ready for toppings!

PIZZA DOUGH

PREP TIME: 15 minutes
RESTING TIME: 1½ hours

INGREDIENTS
1¼ cups cake flour or superfine 00 flour
1 teaspoon fresh yeast
½ teaspoon salt
6 tablespoons lukewarm water
1 teaspoon olive oil

1. Add the flour, yeast, and salt to a mixing bowl. Stir well, making sure to evenly distribute the yeast throughout.

2. Pour in the warm water, and stir quickly. Let rest for a few minutes.

3. Knead vigorously for 5 to 8 minutes. Add the olive oil, and knead it in for another 2 minutes.

4. Place the dough in a medium bowl, cover with a damp cloth, and let rest for 1 hour.

5. Knead for 2 minutes to deflate. Divide the dough into 2 smaller balls. Cover these, and let rest for another 30 minutes. Dough is ready to be rolled out for you to make your pizzas.

CREAMS

PASTRY CREAM

PREP TIME: 20 minutes

INGREDIENTS
1⅔ cups milk

1 vanilla bean

4 egg yolks

⅓ cup sugar

⅓ cup cornstarch

Pastry cream is a traditional French recipe that serves as the foundation for other cream-based desserts.

1. Pour the milk into a medium saucepan, and warm it over low heat. Split the vanilla bean in half, and use the tip of a paring knife to scrape out the seeds. Add the vanilla seeds and pod to the milk, and steep for about 10 minutes; then remove the pod. Remove the saucepan from heat as soon as the milk starts to steam.

2. Add the egg yolks and sugar to a large heatproof mixing bowl. Whisk them together thoroughly, and then whisk in the cornstarch to obtain a smooth mixture. Gradually pour in the hot milk while continuing to whisk. The pastry cream is almost ready.

3. Transfer the cream back to the saucepan, and warm over medium heat, stirring constantly with a wooden spoon until the cream thickens and the spoon leaves tracks in the cream. Remove the saucepan from heat, and transfer the pastry cream to a large heatproof bowl. Cover tightly with plastic wrap, and let cool to room temperature. Refrigerate until ready to use.

CUSTARD

PREP TIME: 10 minutes

INGREDIENTS

1 cup milk
1 vanilla bean
3 egg yolks
1½ tablespoons sugar

1. Pour the milk into a medium saucepan, and warm it over low heat. Split the vanilla bean in half, and use the tip of a paring knife to scrape out the seeds. Add the vanilla seeds and pod to the milk, and steep for about 10 minutes; then remove the pod. Remove the saucepan from heat as soon as the milk starts to steam.

2. Add the egg yolks and sugar to a large heatproof mixing bowl. Whisk them together thoroughly to obtain a smooth mixture. Gradually pour in the hot milk while continuing to whisk. Transfer the resulting mixture back to the saucepan over low heat, stirring constantly with a wooden spoon until the custard thickens. Remove the saucepan from heat, and transfer the custard to a large heatproof bowl. Cover tightly with plastic wrap, and let cool to room temperature. Refrigerate until ready to use.

FRENCH BUTTERCREAM

PREP TIME: 15 minutes

INGREDIENTS

1 cup sugar
3½ tablespoons water
2 eggs plus 2 egg yolks
¾ cup plus 2 tablespoons softened butter, in pieces

Optional flavorings:
Vanilla extract, matcha powder, or cocoa powder

EQUIPMENT

Cooking thermometer
Hand mixer

1. Add the sugar and water to a medium saucepan. Over medium heat, dissolve the sugar in the water to form a syrup. Add the eggs and egg yolks to a large heatproof mixing bowl, and beat with a hand mixer on a low setting.

2. Check the temperature with a cooking thermometer. When the syrup reaches 250°F, remove it from heat, and pour it down the side of the mixing bowl containing the eggs. Continue beating until the syrup is completely combined with the eggs and the action of beating has cooled the mixture. Gradually add and beat in the softened butter. If you want to flavor your cream, now is the time: You can add some vanilla extract, matcha powder, or cocoa powder. Stop mixing as soon as the flavoring is mixed in—overmixing will break the buttercream, and you may have to start over.

3. Tightly cover the buttercream with plastic wrap, and refrigerate until ready to use.

ALMOND CREAM

PREP TIME: 10 minutes

INGREDIENTS

¼ cup butter, at room temperature

¼ cup sugar

2 eggs

½ cup almond flour

1. Cream together the butter and sugar in a large mixing bowl, to completely incorporate the sugar. Add the first egg, and whisk it in. Whisk in the second egg, followed by the almond flour.

2. Your almond cream is ready! Fill tart crusts with it, and bake.

WHIPPED CREAM

PREP TIME: 10 minutes

INGREDIENTS

2 cups heavy whipping cream

Scant ½ cup powdered sugar

Making whipped cream is easy if you know the trick: Start with very cold whipping cream and also a cold mixing bowl and whisk.

1. Place the mixing bowl and whisk (or the beaters of your electric mixer) in the freezer for several minutes until very cold.

2. Add the whipping cream and powdered sugar to the mixing bowl, and whisk vigorously until the whipped cream is firm and forms a peak at the end of your whisk.

COMMONLY USED PIPING TIPS

ROUND TIP OR PLAIN TIP

The round opening of these tips, available in different diameters, is useful for making dots, balls, filigree, and writing, or for forming macaron shells.

STAR TIP

These tips have serrated openings of different diameters. They're used to form stars, flowers, and borders, and they can be used to create round patterns with grooves.

PETAL TIP

The opening is shaped like a teardrop. These tips are perfect for making roses and flowers, as well as ribbons and arches.

FLUTED TIP

Use these tips to make beautiful many-sided stars or to frost cakes and cupcakes.

ICINGS AND FROSTINGS

When you ice a pastry, you coat it with a glossy layer to make it more tantalizing and visually appealing. Use icing to add mystery to a cake or to transform an ordinary dessert into a showstopper. Here are a few commonly used icings.

CHOCOLATE ICING

PREP TIME: 15 minutes
RESTING TIME: 1 hour

INGREDIENTS

7 ounces dark chocolate (70% cocoa)
⅓ cup unsalted butter, at room temperature
1 tablespoon honey

1. Crush the chocolate in a bowl, and set it over a double boiler. Add the butter and honey. Melt over low heat, using a wooden spoon to combine the ingredients until they're smooth and glossy. If the mixture seems too thick, you can add more butter. Remove the saucepan from heat, and let cool.

2. Your icing is ready to use when it reaches a temperature of 85°F (lukewarm to the touch). Place the cake you want to ice on a wire rack above a tray. Use a ladle to pour the icing over the cake, starting from the center. Pour generously to make sure the cake is completely covered. Refrigerate the cake for 1 hour, to allow the icing to set.

ROYAL ICING

PREP TIME: 5 minutes

INGREDIENTS

1¾ cups powdered sugar

1 pasteurized egg white

Juice of ½ lemon

1. Put the powdered sugar in a medium mixing bowl.

2. Add the egg white, and stir to completely combine. Stir in the lemon juice until you have a smooth, glossy icing. Your royal icing is ready!

LEMON GLAZE

PREP TIME: 5 minutes

INGREDIENTS

1 cup powdered sugar

Juice of 1 lemon

1. Put the powdered sugar in a medium mixing bowl. Stir in the lemon juice to obtain a thick white glaze. Pour the glaze over your cake or pastry.

CREAM CHEESE FROSTING

PREP TIME: 5 minutes

INGREDIENTS

3½ ounces cream cheese or mascarpone

¼ cup softened butter

1 tablespoon powdered sugar

1. Add the cream cheese (or mascarpone), butter, and powdered sugar to a medium mixing bowl, and stir until smooth and very creamy. Your frosting is ready!

MIRROR GLAZE

Getting mirror glaze right requires some technique and a bit of practice. When you succeed, you'll end up with a mouthwatering glaze that's glossy and reflective. You can make a mirror glaze with dark chocolate or white chocolate. This recipe uses white couverture chocolate colored red.

PREP TIME: 15 minutes

EQUIPMENT

Cooking thermometer

Immersion blender

INGREDIENTS

5 sheets gelatin

1 cup sugar

⅓ cup plus 1½ tablespoons water

⅔ cup light corn syrup

7 ounces white couverture chocolate wafers

Scant ½ cup condensed milk

1 tablespoon water-soluble red food coloring

1. Rehydrate the gelatin sheets by soaking them in a medium bowl of cold water for 5 to 10 minutes.

2. Make a sugar syrup: Add the sugar, water, and light corn syrup to a medium saucepan. Bring to a boil, and cook until the syrup reaches a temperature of 220°F.

3. Add the chocolate wafers to a large heatproof mixing bowl, and pour the hot syrup over them. Add the condensed milk. Drain the gelatin sheets, and wring out the excess water; add them to the bowl with the chocolate, syrup, and condensed milk.

4. Use an immersion blender to blend for 30 seconds: Make sure to position the blender at the bottom of the bowl instead of near the top, to prevent air bubbles from getting into the glaze. Add the food coloring, and blend for a few seconds to distribute evenly. Your mirror glaze is almost ready. Wait until it cools to 90°F before using it on a cake.

5. Place your cake on a wire rack above a tray. Use a ladle to pour the icing over the cake, starting from the center. Pour generously, to make sure the cake is completely covered. Refrigerate for 1 hour to allow the glaze to set.

If you prefer not to use food coloring, feel free to replace the white chocolate with dark couverture chocolate (70% cocoa).

SPONGE CAKES

JOCONDE SPONGE CAKE

PREP TIME: 10 minutes
COOK TIME: 10 minutes

INGREDIENTS

¾ cup plus 2 tablespoons powdered sugar

1 cup almond flour

3 eggs plus 2 egg whites, divided

¼ cup plus ½ tablespoon all-purpose flour

1 tablespoon granulated sugar

EQUIPMENT

Hand mixer or whisk

1. Preheat the oven to 350°F. Combine the powdered sugar and almond flour in a medium mixing bowl. Beat the 3 eggs in a separate large mixing bowl, and then stir in the sugar–almond flour mixture until the batter is smooth and flows in thick ribbons. Stir in the all-purpose flour, and set aside while you make French meringue.

2. Place the 2 egg whites in a large mixing bowl. Use a hand mixer or a whisk to beat the egg whites until bubbles start to form. When the egg whites have doubled in volume, add the granulated sugar; continue beating until the mixture forms stiff peaks. Use a spatula to carefully fold the egg white mixture into the batter from the previous step.

3. Line a sheet pan with parchment paper. Pour the batter into the pan, and bake for 10 minutes.

GENOISE SPONGE CAKE

PREP TIME: 10 minutes
COOK TIME: 10 minutes

INGREDIENTS

YIELD: MAKES 1 SHEET OF GENOISE SPONGE CAKE

4 eggs

½ cup plus 2 tablespoons sugar

Salt

1 cup flour

EQUIPMENT

Hand mixer or whisk

1. Preheat the oven to 350°F.

2. Bring a large pot of water to a boil. Add the eggs and sugar to a double boiler. Use a whisk or a hand mixer to beat the eggs and sugar until frothy.

3. Remove the mixing bowl from the double boiler. Add a pinch of salt and the flour, a little at a time, carefully folding in the dry ingredients with a spatula in a bottom-to-top motion, to avoid deflating the frothy egg mixture. When you have a smooth batter, spread it out evenly on a sheet pan lined with parchment paper. Bake for 10 minutes.

CHOCOLATE

CHOCOLATE SAUCE

PREP TIME: 10 minutes

INGREDIENTS

5½ ounces baking chocolate

1¼ cups water

½ cup sugar

⅔ cup crème fraîche

1. Crush the chocolate, and put it in a medium saucepan along with the water, sugar, and crème fraîche. Bring to a boil over medium heat, and stir until completely combined. Maintain a gentle boil for 5 minutes, stirring constantly.

2. Your sauce is perfect when it is smooth and glossy and coats the back of your spoon. Serve right away, or transfer to a container and cover the surface with plastic wrap. The chocolate sauce will keep for up to 5 days in the refrigerator.

TYPES OF CHOCOLATE

Chocolate can be divided into three categories: dark chocolate, milk chocolate, and white chocolate.

MILK CHOCOLATE

Milk chocolate is made of cocoa mass, cocoa butter, sugar, and powdered milk. It is smooth on the palate and may even have caramel notes. Milk chocolate is also sweeter than dark chocolate.

DARK CHOCOLATE

Dark chocolate contains a minimum of 35% cocoa (and up to 99%). The remainder is mainly cocoa butter and sugar. Various other ingredients and flavorings can also be added. The higher the cocoa content, the greater the health benefits to eating chocolate (which contains fiber, antioxidants, magnesium, and iron).

WHITE CHOCOLATE

White chocolate consists mainly of cocoa butter, sugar, and milk. This product is chocolate in name only: It does not contain cocoa mass.

TEMPERING CHOCOLATE

Tempering chocolate involves cycling the chocolate through different temperatures. The process crystallizes the fats, and it organizes and evenly distributes the atoms in the chocolate. Tempered chocolate is glossier, snaps when broken, and is considerably easier to work with.

Note that chocolatiers prefer to start with couverture chocolate.

INGREDIENTS

10½ ounces couverture chocolate

EQUIPMENT

Double boiler
Cooking thermometer

1. Using a double boiler, melt 7 ounces couverture chocolate over a medium saucepan, taking care not to exceed 130°F.

2. Chop an additional 3½ ounces chocolate, and stir it into the melted chocolate while reducing the heat and stirring. This reduces the temperature of the chocolate in a controlled way.

3. When the chocolate reaches 82°F, warm it again until it measures 88°F to 90°F. At this temperature, dark chocolate is ready to use.

The ideal temperature depends on the type of chocolate:

- For white chocolate: Melt and heat to 110°F, cool to 78°F, and reheat to 84°F before using.

- For milk chocolate: Melt and heat to 110°F, cool to 80°F, and reheat to 86°F.

TEMPERATURE

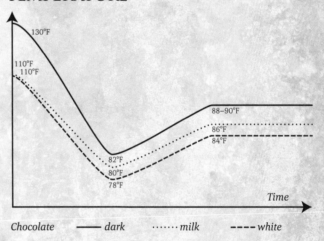

Chocolate ——— dark ········· milk ----- white

SYRUPS AND DESSERT SAUCES

SYRUP

Syrup is a liquid made by dissolving sugar in water. Specific types of syrups work for poaching fruits, soaking cake layers, cooking eggs (as in Italian meringue), and so on. Different proportions of sugar and water result in the different types of syrup.

BASIC SYRUP

INGREDIENTS

4 cups water

5 cups sugar

1. Add the water and sugar to a large saucepan, bring to a boil, and boil for 2 minutes. Remove saucepan from heat. Your syrup is ready.

LIGHT SYRUP

INGREDIENTS

4 cups water

1 cup sugar

1. Add the water and sugar to a large saucepan, bring to a boil, and boil for 2 minutes. Remove saucepan from heat. Your syrup is ready.

2. You can add fruits or herbs such as verbena, mint leaves, or dried hibiscus flowers to flavor your syrup. Just remember to strain before using.

CARAMEL

Caramel is, by definition, a stage in cooking sugar after the temperature reaches 320°F.

LIQUID CARAMEL

PREP TIME: 5 minutes
COOK TIME: 10 minutes

INGREDIENTS

1½ cups sugar

3 tablespoons lemon juice

10 tablespoons water, divided

1. Add the sugar, lemon juice, and 3 tablespoons water to a medium heavy-bottomed saucepan. Melt the sugar over medium heat until the syrup takes on an amber color. Add the remaining 7 tablespoons water, and cook for another 2 minutes. Your liquid caramel is ready!

SALTED BUTTER CARAMEL SAUCE

PREP TIME: 10 minutes
COOK TIME: 10 minutes

INGREDIENTS

⅔ cup cream

¾ cup sugar

⅔ cup water

1 tablespoon salted butter, in pieces

1. Pour the cream into a small saucepan, and bring it to a gentle boil over medium heat.

2. In a separate medium saucepan, heat the sugar with the water until the mixture takes on an amber color. Remove the caramel from heat, and gradually pour in the boiling cream, stirring vigorously as you pour so that it mixes in.

3. Stir in the butter until you have a thick sauce. Transfer to a container, and let cool.

SPREADS AND BUTTERS

CHOCOLATE HAZELNUT SPREAD

PREP TIME: 25 minutes
COOK TIME: 15 minutes

EQUIPMENT
Blender

INGREDIENTS

1½ cups whole hazelnuts

⅔ cup granulated sugar

1⅓ cups powdered sugar

5½ ounces milk chocolate

¼ cup powdered milk

3 tablespoons dark cocoa powder

1 tablespoon sunflower oil

1. Toast the hazelnuts: Preheat the oven to 350°F. Place the hazelnuts on a baking sheet, and bake for 15 minutes. While the hazelnuts are baking, set a clean cloth on a plate nearby. When the hazelnuts are toasted, transfer the hot nuts to the cloth, taking care not to burn yourself. Rub the hazelnuts with the cloth to remove their skins. Set aside.

2. Make a dry caramel: In a medium heavy-bottomed saucepan, melt ⅓ of the granulated sugar over low heat, without stirring. Then add another third, and melt again, without stirring. Finally, add the remaining granulated sugar, and again, let it melt without stirring. Your caramel is ready when it turns a blonde color. Use a silicone baking mat or line a baking sheet with parchment paper, and pour the caramel onto it. Let the caramel cool and harden, and then crush it.

3. Make the hazelnut caramel: Add half the toasted hazelnuts to a blender. Add the caramel pieces, and blend until the mixture liquefies. Transfer to a bowl, and set aside.

4. Make the hazelnut butter: Add the remaining hazelnuts to the blender, along with the powdered sugar. Blend for several minutes to form a dense, smooth butter.

5. Melt the milk chocolate in a medium saucepan, double boiler, or microwave. Add the melted chocolate to the blender along with the hazelnut butter. Add the hazelnut caramel, powdered milk, cocoa powder, and sunflower oil. Blend the ingredients by pulsing for 5 to 10 seconds at a time. The more you blend, the runnier it will become. Continue blending until the spread reaches your desired consistency. Transfer to an airtight container, and enjoy within 7 days.

SPECULOOS COOKIE BUTTER

PREP TIME: 10 minutes

COOK TIME: 5 minutes

EQUIPMENT

Immersion blender

INGREDIENTS

7 ounces speculoos cookies

1 cup evaporated milk

1 teaspoon honey

1 teaspoon cinnamon

1. In a large heatproof mixing bowl, use an immersion blender to crush the speculoos cookies into powder.

2. In a medium saucepan, warm the evaporated milk, honey, and cinnamon over medium heat. Stir well to thoroughly combine the ingredients, and then pour the hot mixture into the mixing bowl with the speculoos cookie powder.

3. Use a spatula or a wooden spoon to mix until you have a smooth spread. Transfer to a glass jar. Your homemade speculoos cookie spread is ready!

ANKO PASTE

PREP TIME: 10 minutes

RESTING TIME: 2 hours

COOK TIME: 1¼ hours

INGREDIENTS

7 ounces dried adzuki beans

3 cups mineral water

¾ cup plus 2 tablespoons sugar

Salt

1. Soak the adzuki beans for 2 hours in a bowl of cold tap water.

2. Drain, and transfer the beans to a large saucepan. Add more tap water to cover the beans, and bring to a gentle boil. Cook for 5 minutes. Then drain the beans and repeat this step with a fresh pot of tap water.

3. By this time, the beans should have lost any bitterness. Pour the mineral water into the saucepan, and add the beans back in. Cook at a gentle boil for 50 minutes to 1 hour, until the beans are soft all the way through.

4. Remove from heat, and let the beans soak in the hot water for another 10 minutes. Drain off a third of the cooking water, and add the sugar and a pinch of salt.

5. Turn the heat back to medium, and simmer for 15 to 20 minutes, stirring frequently. You want the mixture to reduce until you have a nice mashed consistency—not too runny, but still slightly syrupy. Your red bean paste is ready!

PISTACHIO BUTTER

PREP TIME: 10 minutes
COOK TIME: 15 minutes

EQUIPMENT

Cooking thermometer
Blender

INGREDIENTS

1 cup raw shelled pistachios

⅓ cup sugar

3½ tablespoons water

⅓ cup almond flour

3 drops almond extract

1 tablespoon peanut oil
(or sunflower or grapeseed oil)

1. Toast the pistachios: Preheat the oven to 300°F. Line a baking sheet with parchment paper. Arrange the pistachios on the baking sheet, and bake for 15 minutes.

2. Make a syrup: In a small saucepan, melt the sugar into the water. Bring the mixture to a boil, using a cooking thermometer to monitor the temperature. When it reaches 250°F, remove the saucepan from heat.

3. Drop the toasted pistachios into the saucepan with the syrup. Stir with a wooden spoon to thoroughly coat the pistachios with syrup.

4. Transfer the syrupy pistachios to a blender, and add the almond flour and almond extract. Blend for 2 minutes, pausing from time to time. Add the oil, and blend for another 10 seconds. Your pistachio butter is ready!

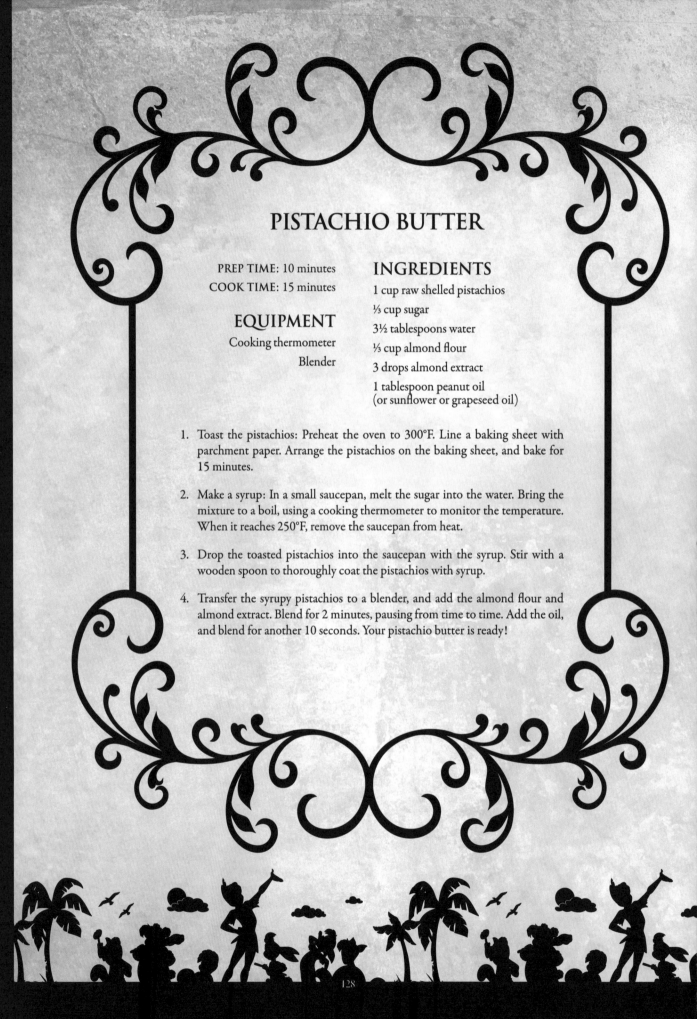

MERINGUES

ITALIAN MERINGUE

PREP TIME: 15 minutes
COOK TIME: 10 minutes

EQUIPMENT

Stand mixer
Cooking thermometer

INGREDIENTS

2 squeezes of lemon juice, divided
1¼ cups sugar
⅔ cup water
4 pasteurized egg whites

1. Make a syrup: Add 1 squeeze of the lemon juice and the sugar and water to a small saucepan. Warm over medium heat to a temperature of 240°F.

2. Pour the egg whites into the bowl of a stand mixer. Add the remaining squeeze of lemon juice, and beat for 2 minutes on a slow setting. Increase the speed to medium, and continue beating the eggs until frothy. With the mixer running, slowly drizzle in the sugar syrup. Continue to beat for another 5 minutes.

3. Increase the speed to high, and beat the mixture until the bowl is cool to the touch and the meringue forms soft peaks. Your Italian meringue is ready! You can use it to garnish a lemon tart or a baked Alaska.

FRENCH MERINGUE

PREP TIME: 15 minutes
COOK TIME: 1 hour

EQUIPMENT

Stand mixer

INGREDIENTS

4 egg whites
1 squeeze of lemon juice
1 cup sugar

1. Preheat the oven to 200°F.

2. Pour the egg whites into the bowl of a stand mixer. Add the lemon juice, and beat for 2 minutes on a slow setting. Increase the speed to medium, and slowly add in the sugar all at once; then beat for another 5 minutes. Your French meringue is ready when it forms soft peaks. Transfer the meringue to a piping bag, and set aside.

3. Line a baking sheet with parchment paper. Pipe the meringue onto the baking sheet, and bake for 1 hour. When done, it should be dry in the center.

ICE CREAMS

VANILLA ICE CREAM

PREP TIME: 10 minutes
COOK TIME: 5 minutes
RESTING TIME: 15 minutes
CHURNING TIME: 5 to 10 minutes

EQUIPMENT
Cooking thermometer

INGREDIENTS
2 cups whole milk

1 cup heavy whipping cream

2 vanilla beans

8 egg yolks

½ cup plus 1 tablespoon sugar

1 teaspoon fleur de sel

2 pounds ice cubes or crushed ice

1¼ cups coarse salt

Nothing is easier than whipping up your own homemade ice cream—it only takes a few minutes, and it doesn't require a lot of special equipment.

1. Make a custard: Pour the milk and whipping cream into a large saucepan. Split the vanilla beans in half lengthwise, and use the tip of a paring knife to scrape out the seeds. Add the vanilla pods and seeds to the saucepan. Bring to a boil; then remove the saucepan from heat. Leave the vanilla to steep in the milk for 15 minutes, and then remove the pods.

2. Meanwhile, add the egg yolks, sugar, and fleur de sel to a large heatproof mixing bowl. Beat vigorously with a whisk until the mixture turns lighter in color. Add the vanilla-infused milk a third at a time, whisking continuously.

3. Pour the contents of your mixing bowl back into the saucepan, and warm over medium heat. While stirring constantly with a figure-eight motion, heat the mixture to a temperature of 180°F. Monitor it using a cooking thermometer, and take

care not to exceed this temperature—otherwise, the eggs will overcook and the ice cream will be ruined. The custard is ready when it coats the back of a spoon.

4. Chill the custard: Pour the ice into a large mixing bowl, and add the coarse salt. Mix the salt and ice, and then set a smaller mixing bowl down into it. Pour your custard into the smaller bowl, and begin whisking it or stirring with a silicone spatula for 5 to 10 minutes. The salt will reduce the temperature of the ice from about 28°F to 3°F, which is perfect for churning your ice cream by hand.

5. When you have stirred the ice cream base in the cold bowl for several minutes, you will see it thicken and transform into a delicious ice cream! Enjoy it right away, or store it in an airtight container in the freezer.

CHOCOLATE ICE CREAM

PREP TIME: 20 minutes
COOK TIME: 10 minutes
RESTING TIME: 12 hours
CHURNING TIME: 25 minutes

EQUIPMENT

Cooking thermometer
Ice cream maker
Immersion blender
Heatproof strainer

INGREDIENTS

2 cups whole milk

1 cup crème fraîche

3½ ounces dark baking chocolate, crushed

1 cup plus 1 tablespoon dark cocoa powder

1 tablespoon honey

3 large egg yolks

¾ cup superfine sugar

Make your ice cream base the day before you plan to serve the ice cream.

1. Set up your station: Prepare a large bowl of cold water and ice cubes. Place a large mixing bowl in the refrigerator.

2. Pour the milk and crème fraîche into a large saucepan, and warm over medium heat. Use a cooking thermometer to monitor the temperature. When it reaches 140°F, add the chocolate, cocoa powder, and honey. Continue cooking while you whisk together the ingredients. Reduce heat to low.

3. Add the egg yolks and sugar to a large heat-proof mixing bowl. Whisk until the mixture is yellow and frothy.

4. When the chocolate mixture has cooled to 110°F, pour it into the egg yolks while stirring continuously. When the ingredients are all thoroughly combined, transfer the resulting mixture to the saucepan, and warm over medium heat to a temperature of 185°F. Maintain this temperature for at least 3 minutes, to pasteurize the ingredients and kill any natural bacteria that may develop.

5. Remove the mixing bowl from the refrigerator. Strain your chocolate ice cream base into the chilled mixing bowl. Immediately set the mixing bowl over the bowl of water and ice cubes that you have prepared. Whisk the ice cream base, to stop the egg yolks from cooking and reduce its temperature to 40°F. Cover tightly with plastic wrap, and refrigerate overnight or for at least 12 hours. (This resting time helps the chocolate release its full flavor.)

6. Your ice cream base is ready.

7. The following day, use an immersion blender to blend your ice cream base for at least 4 minutes. Transfer it to the ice cream maker. Churn for 25 minutes. Meanwhile, clean the mixing bowl and place it in the freezer.

8. After 25 minutes of churning, transfer the chocolate ice cream into the chilled mixing bowl. Cover tightly with plastic wrap, and freeze for at least 2 hours. Your ice cream is ready to eat!

SEASONAL FRUITS AND NUTS

SPRING

Alpine strawberries	Currants	Mangoes	Passion fruit	Tomatoes
Apricots	Kiwis	Melons	Peaches	Watermelons
Avocados	Lemons	Nectarines	Raspberries	
Bananas	Lychees	Papayas	Strawberries	

SUMMER

Almonds	Cherries	Greengage plums	Nectarines	Raspberries
Alpine strawberries	Chestnuts	Hazelnuts	Papayas	Strawberries
Apricots	Cranberries	Lemons	Passion fruit	Tomatoes
Bananas	Currants	Lychees	Peaches	Watermelons
Blackberries	Damson plums	Mangoes	Pears	
Blackcurrants	Dates	Melons	Plums	
Blueberries	Figs	Mirabelle plums	Quinces	

AUTUMN

Apples	Dates	Kumquats	Papayas	Pomegranates
Avocados	Figs	Lemons	Passion fruit	Quinces
Bananas	Grapefruits	Lychees	Pears	Walnuts
Chestnuts	Grapes	Mandarins	Persimmons	
Clementines	Hazelnuts	Mangoes	Pineapples	
Damson plums	Kiwis	Oranges	Plums	

WINTER

Apples	Dates	Lychees	Papayas	Pineapples
Avocados	Grapefruits	Mandarins	Passion fruit	Pomegranates
Bananas	Kiwis	Mangoes	Pears	
Clementines	Lemons	Oranges	Persimmons	

FRY STATION SAFETY TIPS

If you're making something that requires deep frying, here are some important tips to prevent any kitchen fires:

- If you don't have a dedicated deep fryer, use a Dutch oven or a high-walled sauté pan.

- Never have too much oil in the pan! You don't want hot oil spilling out as soon as you put the food in.

- Only use a suitable cooking oil, like canola, peanut, or vegetable oil.

- Always keep track of the oil temperature with a thermometer—350°F to 375°F should do the trick.

- Never put too much food in the pan at the same time!

- Never put wet food in the pan. It will splatter and may cause burns.

- Always have a lid nearby to cover the pan in case it starts to spill over or catch fire. A properly rated fire extinguisher is also great to have on hand in case of emergencies.

- Never leave the pan unattended, and never let children near the pan.

- Never, ever put your face, hand, or any other body part in the hot oil.

KITCHEN MEASUREMENTS

CUPS	TABLESPOONS	TEASPOONS	FLUID OUNCES
¹⁄₁₆ cup	1 Tbsp	3 tsp	½ fl oz
⅛ cup	2 Tbsp	6 tsp	1 fl oz
¼ cup	4 Tbsp	12 tsp	2 fl oz
⅓ cup	5½ Tbsp	16 tsp	2⅔ fl oz
½ cup	8 Tbsp	24 tsp	4 fl oz
⅔ cup	10⅔ Tbsp	32 tsp	5⅓ fl oz
¾ cup	12 Tbsp	36 tsp	6 fl oz
1 cup	16 Tbsp	48 tsp	8 fl oz

GLOSSARY

BAKING SODA
A chemical substance with many useful properties for cooking. Baking soda is used to create rise in baked goods.

BATTER
A mixture of ingredients (cake batter, for example).

BEAT
Vigorously whisk a preparation to thoroughly mix ingredients or increase volume.

BLANCH
Briefly scald almonds, hazelnuts, or pistachios to make their skins easier to remove.

CANDY (VERB)
Infuse fruit in a sugar syrup to preserve it or make candied fruit.

COOKIE CUTTER
Made of metal or thick plastic, cookie cutters come in many different shapes (such as circle or square). They are pressed into dough (pastry, cookie, or pie crust) to cut it into shaped pieces.

CRUSH
Smash or cut fruits, vegetables, nuts, or chocolate into uneven pieces.

DOUBLE BOILER
Cooking technique that consists of placing a vessel containing an ingredient or mixture above a bath of boiling water to cook, melt (chocolate, for example), or warm it without risk of burning.

DUST
Sprinkle flour over a surface (such as your work surface) to prevent ingredients from sticking to it.

FLAMBÉ
Pour alcohol over a dessert, sauce, or fruit, and then light it on fire. This can be dangerous, so take all necessary precautions and have children stand back when flambéing.

GELATIN
Available in sheet or powdered form, gelatin is an animal-derived gelling agent used in making candies, marshmallows, and icings. It can be replaced with other types of gelling agents, such as agar, which is plant based.

ICE (VERB)

Cover the surface of a pastry with icing.

Make a pastry glossy by pouring syrup over it after removing it from the oven, or by covering it with powdered sugar that is then melted in the oven.

LIGHT CORN SYRUP

A thick, viscous, colorless liquid derived from cornstarch. It is used in pastry making to slow the crystallization of sugar and lower its freezing point. It is found in recipes for soft caramels and glossy icings.

LINE

Cover the sides and bottom of a baking mold with flour, butter, powdered sugar, or a sheet of parchment paper. Preparing a mold by lining it makes it easier to remove items after baking. Also refers to covering the bottom of a pie plate or tart pan with crust.

MASCARPONE

A fairly rich Italian cheese made from cow's milk. It is usually used in traditional tiramisu but also appears in some cheesecake recipes.

MATCHA

Finely ground green tea powder. Matcha is a rich source of vitamins and minerals and offers many health benefits. It is a unique shade of green and can be used to add both flavor and color to a cream-based dessert or cake. For this purpose, I recommend using organic culinary matcha.

MIXING BOWL

Large round-bottomed bowl usually made of stainless steel.

GLOSSARY

MOISTEN

Allow liquid to soak into a cake or cookie, to soften or flavor it.

PASTRY RING

Stainless-steel ring that can be used as a mold or a cookie cutter.

RIBBON STAGE

Describes a thick cream or batter that flows slowly off a spoon and stays suspended on the surface for a few moments before gradually disappearing.

ROLL OUT DOUGH

Use a rolling pin to flatten out your dough to your desired thickness on a floured work surface.

ROSE WATER

Product of distilling rose petals. It has a concentrated rose fragrance and flavor and is widely used in Middle Eastern cuisine.

SEPARATE AN EGG

Remove the egg yolk from the egg white.

SET ASIDE

Keep a mixture or ingredient for later use while preparing a recipe.

SIFT

Pass a dry ingredient, such as flour or sugar, through a sieve or sifter, to eliminate lumps.

SILICONE SPATULA

A flexible spatula used to scrape the sides of a container to recover as much as possible of what it contains.

SOFTENED BUTTER

Butter that has been beaten to a creamy consistency.

SPRINGFORM PAN

A cake pan with high sides, either smooth or fluted, and a removable bottom. It is used for many baked desserts, such as genoise and cheesecake.

TOAST

Brown a dry ingredient, such as coffee beans, hazelnuts, or almonds, without fat to release its flavors.

WELL

A hole made in flour or other dry ingredients to pour the wet ingredients into before mixing.

ZEST

Use a zester or paring knife to remove the zest from a citrus fruit. The zest can be used to flavor a cream or mixture.

INDEX

A

ALMOND CREAM
Adventure Is Out There Ice Cream 67
Transformation Spell Cake.................28

ALMONDS, SLICED
Be Our Guest Paris-Brest....................20
Beastly Crêpes Suzette 24
Legendary Sticky Rice....................103

ANKO PASTE
Sweet Bao 72

APPLES
Wishing Apple..............................14

B

BANANAS
Adventure Is Out There Ice Cream 67
Bananas Foster for Louis.....................30
Legendary Sticky Rice....................103
Pizza from the Great Beyond 105

BLACKBERRIES
Lucky Cat Café Neko Muffins..............58
Mousse for Jack-Jack........................95

BLUEBERRIES
Pizza from the Great Beyond 105
Royal Wedding Cake....................... 32
Transformation Spell Cake................ 28

BREAD, SANDWICH
It's Jammed! Explosive PB&J 78

BUTTER, ALMOND
Pizza from the Great Beyond 105

BUTTER, PISTACHIO
Breakfast Time Porridge 19

C

CARDAMOM
Bare Necessities Lassi.......................52

CARROTS
Carrot Pops 88

CHERRIES, CANDIED
One Extraterrestrial Bite Cake 76
Portorosso Cannoli.........................68

CHOCOLATE, DARK
A Cake for Cleo 38
Mama Madrigal's Buñuelos 71

CHOCOLATE, WHITE
Pizza from the Great Beyond 105

CHOCOLATE CHIPS, MILK
Tower Cookies.............................. 26

CHOCOLATE HAZELNUT BUTTER
Adventure Is Out There Ice Cream 67

CINNAMON
Bananas Foster for Louis.....................30
Bare Necessities Lassi.......................52
Hercules Fan Cola..........................98

COCOA POWDER, DARK
Adventure Is Out There Ice Cream 67
One Extraterrestrial Bite Cake 76
Randall's Be My Pal Cupcakes.............91

COINTREAU
A Cake for Cleo 38

CORNSTARCH
Be Our Guest Paris-Brest...................20
Mama Madrigal's Buñuelos 71
Roquefort's Delight 54

F

FETA
Mama Madrigal's Buñuelos 71

FLOUR, ALMOND
Transformation Spell Cake................28

FLOUR, CASSAVA
Mama Madrigal's Buñuelos 71

FLOUR, DUMPLING
Sweet Bao 72

FOOD COLORING, GREEN
Royal Wedding Cake........................32

FOOD COLORING, RED
Wishing Apple...............................14

G

GINGER, CANDIED
Iced Royal Crown Cake 106
Penny's Cookies 62

GINGER, FRESH
Carrot Pops 88
Hercules Fan Cola..........................98

GINGER, GROUND
Penny's Cookies 62

GRAND MARNIER
Beastly Crêpes Suzette 24

H

HAZELNUTS, SHELLED
A Cake for Cleo 38

HIBISCUS FLOWERS, DRIED
Kumandra Iced Tea...................... 100

HONEY, LAVENDER
Breakfast Time Porridge 19

HONEY, LIQUID
Adventure Is Out There Ice Cream 67
Bare Necessities Lassi...................... 52
Carrot Pops 88
It's Jammed! Explosive PB&J 78
Mama Madrigal's Buñuelos 71
Marigold Bridge Pan de Muerto 60
Pancake Breakfast 64
Penny's Cookies 62

HONEY, THISTLE
Transformation Spell Cake.................28

I

ICE CREAM, VANILLA
Bananas Foster for Louis...................30

J

JAM, APRICOT
Breakfast Time Porridge 19

JAM, STRAWBERRY
Doughnuts for Lady........................48
It's Jammed! Explosive PB&J 78

JASMINE
Kumandra Iced Tea...................... 100

JUICE, POMEGRANATE
Hercules Fan Cola..........................98

K

KIWIS
Pizza from the Great Beyond 105

L

LEMONGRASS
Kumandra Iced Tea 100

LIME
Legendary Sticky Rice 103

LIQUEUR, ORANGE
Beastly Crêpes Suzette 24

M

MACADAMIA NUTS
Tower Cookies 26

MANGOES
Bare Necessities Lassi 52
Legendary Sticky Rice 103

MARMALADE, SEVILLE ORANGE
Iced Royal Crown Cake 106

MASCARPONE
Randall's Be My Pal Cupcakes 91
Royal Wedding Cake 32

MILK, ALMOND
Bare Necessities Lass 52
Breakfast Time Porridge 19

MILK, COCONUT
Legendary Sticky Rice 103

MINT
Hercules Fan Cola 98

O

OATS, ROLLED
Breakfast Time Porridge 19

OIL, COCONUT
Adventure Is Out There Ice Cream 67

ORANGES
Beastly Crêpes Suzette 24
A Cake for Cleo 38
Hercules Fan Cola 98
Iced Royal Crown Cake 106
Marigold Bridge Pan de Muerto 60

ORANGE BLOSSOM WATER
Marigold Bridge Pan de Muerto 60

P

PEANUTS
It's Jammed! Explosive PB&J 78

PECANS
Bananas Foster for Louis 30
Regular Ole Living Pecan Pie 80

PEPPERS, CHILE
Kumandra Iced Tea 100

PISTACHIOS
Breakfast Time Porridge 19
Portorosso Cannoli 68

PRALINE PASTE
Be Our Guest Paris-Brest 20

R

RASPBERRIES
Royal Wedding Cake 32

RICE, STICKY
Legendary Sticky Rice....................103

RICOTTA
Portorosso Cannoli..........................68

ROSE WATER
Royal Wedding Cake......................32

RUM, DARK
Bananas Foster for Louis...................30

S

SODA, LEMON-LIME
Hercules Fan Cola..........................98

SPECULOOS COOKIES
Bananas Foster for Louis...................30
Carrot Pops.................................88

STAR ANISE
Bare Necessities Lassi......................52
Hercules Fan Cola..........................98

STRAWBERRIES
Pawpsicles..................................86
Royal Wedding Cake......................32

SUGAR, PALM
Kumandra Iced Tea......................100

SYRUP, LAVENDER
Mousse for Jack-Jack......................95

SYRUP, MAPLE
Pancake Breakfast..........................64
Regular Ole Living Pecan Pie.............80

SYRUP, ROSEMARY
Wishing Apple..............................14

T

TEA, BLACK
Kumandra Iced Tea.......................100

TEA, MATCHA
Lucky Cat Café Neko Muffins.............58

V

VANILLA BEAN
Hercules Fan Cola..........................98
Portorosso Cannoli..........................68
Roquefort's Delight........................54

VANILLA EXTRACT
Adventure Is Out There Ice Cream........67
Beastly Crêpes Suzette.....................24
Everyday Waffles for Not-So-Everyday
    Kids.....................................96
Pancake Breakfast..........................64
Randall's Be My Pal Cupcakes.............91
Regular Ole Living Pecan Pie.............80
Roquefort's Delight........................54
Royal Wedding Cake......................32
Transformation Spell Cake................28

VERBENA, FRESH
Pawpsicles..................................86

W

WAFFLE CONE
Adventure Is Out There Ice Cream........67

Y

YOGURT, PLAIN
Bare Necessities Lassi......................52

Y ou've come to the end of the book—I hope you liked it!

Tradition dictates that I begin my acknowledgments with my dearest Bérengère: None of this could have happened without you—not a single book, not a single adventure to the far reaches of fantasy worlds. We have been meandering through life together for more than ten years now, sharing everything, and I thank you for that. Thank you, too, for being as demanding and dedicated an artistic director as I am—thanks to you, this book is another work of art.

Henri, my son, you recently watched *Robin Hood*, *The Sword in the Stone*, and *Cinderella* for the first time, and you've been singing us the greatest hits from *The Aristocats* for a while now. Your journey has only just begun, and I can't wait until we can bake together. I love you.

Thank you to my parents and my sister for your tireless support, love, and confidence. Dad, the more I think about it, the more I realize that I owe my passion for cooking to one of your apple pies—simple, humble, yet fantastic, seasoned with an expert hand and with the love you have always had for us. Thank you for that spark—thank you for everything.

Thank you, Mehdiya and Nicolas, for recreating my recipes and bringing them to life with your fabulous photography!

Nicolas, I'm delighted to add this book to our growing stack. We should be proud of ourselves!

Thank you to my team, particularly Baptiste, who is my right hand in everything, and whose hard work and eye for detail make my creative work better.

Thank you to everyone who offered me their time, advice, and loans.

Thank you to Catherine, Antoine, and Anne with Hachette Heroes—you know how happy I am to get to work with you, and I hope we'll keep on doing it for many years!

Thank you to everyone at Hachette Heroes who will put this cookbook into your hands and make sure it gets the attention it deserves.

Thank you to everyone at Disney who entrusted me with the keys to the sanctuary— I hope I've proven myself worthy.

And finally, a heartfelt thank you to my dear community—readers, viewers, fans who have been with me from the start, and silent observers. Thank you. Thank you. Thank you. THANK YOU.

Butter is happiness,

Thibaud Villanova
Gastronogeek

The Aristocats is based on a story by Tom Rowe.

The characters in the Disney films *The Rescuers* and *The Rescuers Down Under* are inspired by the books by Margery Sharp, *The Rescuers* and *Miss Bianca*, published by Little, Brown and Company.

The Hundred and One Dalmatians is a novel by Dodie Smith, published by Viking Press.

Photo credits: Adobe Stock (faitotoro, ABCDstock, Nattha99, great19, TWINS DESIGN STUDIO, Сергей Байбак, Denys), Shutterstock (Julietphotography, Tendo, Hein Nouwens), Bérengère Demoncy

Hachette Livre (Hachette Pratique)
58 Rue Jean Bleuzen – 92178 Vanves Cedex France
www.hachette-heroes.com
facebook.com/hachetteheroes
instagram.com/hachetteheroes
Join us on YouTube to continue the adventure:
▶ www.youtube.com/gastronogeek
📘 www.facebook.com/gastronogeek
🐦 www.twitter.com/gastronogeek
📷 www.instagram.com/gastronogeek
www.gastronogeek.com

The publisher is committed to using paper made of natural, renewable, recyclable fibers manufactured from wood grown in sustainably managed forests. Furthermore, the publisher requires its paper suppliers to comply with a recognized environmental certification program.

Managing Editor: Catherine Saunier-Talec
Project Director: Antoine Béon
Project Manager: Anne Vallet
Layout: Bérengère Demoncy
Proofreading: Charlotte Buch-Müller
Printing: Anne-Laure Soyez

PO Box 3088
San Rafael, CA 94912
www.insighteditions.com

📘 Find us on Facebook: www.facebook.com/InsightEditions
📷 Follow us on Instagram: @insighteditions

ISBN: 979-8-88663-563-8

Publisher: Raoul Goff
VP, Group Publisher: Vanessa Lopez
VP, Creative: Chrissy Kwasnik
VP, Manufacturing: Alix Nicholaeff
Art Director: Stuart Smith
Design Manager: Megan Sinead-Harris
Editor: Jennifer Pellman
VP, Senior Executive Project Editor: Vicki Jaeger
Production Associate: Deena Hashem
Senior Production Manager, Subsidiary Rights: Lina s Palma-Temena

ROOTS•PEACE REPLANTED PAPER

Insight Editions, in association with Roots of Peace, will plant two trees for each tree used in the manufacturing of this book. Roots of Peace is an internationally renowned humanitarian organization dedicated to eradicating land mines worldwide and converting war-torn lands into productive farms and wildlife habitats. Roots of Peace will plant two million fruit and nut trees in Afghanistan and provide farmers there with the skills and support necessary for sustainable land use.

Printed in China by LPP

10 9 8 7 6 5 4 3 2 1